Swine and Pearls

Pastor Vendrix Headley

Written Words Publishing LLC
14189 E Dickinson Drive, Unit F
Aurora, Colorado 80014
www.writtenwordspublishing.com

Published by Written Word Publishing LLC June 9, 2023.

ISBN: 978-1-961610-00-2 (paperback)
ISBN: 978-1-961610-01-9 (eBook)

Library of Congress Control Number: 2023910544

Manufactured and printed in the United States of America

Dedication

This book is an essential tribute to my beloved sons, Aniel and Nashon Headley. As you peruse its pages, you will gain invaluable insights and guidance to lead your life in accordance with God's will. This book is not solely intended for my sons but for all young adults seeking love and companionship, specifically focusing on those who have encountered marital difficulties in the past or are currently searching for that special someone.

The sage advice contained in this book will enable you to navigate the complexities of relationships with confidence and ease. Always remember, there is hope and a viable path forward, whether you are seeking a life partner or hoping to repair a current marriage. With God's guidance and a willingness to learn and grow, you can attain the love and happiness you deserve. Thus, I wholeheartedly dedicate this book to every one of you. It will provide you with comfort and clarity, as well as the strength and determination to follow God's plan for your life.

LET THE SEARCH BEGIN

"Whoso findeth a wife findeth a good thing, and obtaineth favour of the Lord" (Proverbs 18:22).

Table of Contents

Love is Beautiful

Love is beautiful

Love is kind

Love is passionate and so are you

Each time your eyes look into mine, you ignite
the fire I cannot hide

My heart glows

My joy flows

And that's how I know that a love like thine is
one of a kind

By Pastor Vendrix Headley

Acknowledgments

Many thanks to the Almighty, the only wise God who is the God of all impossibility. I am humbled by the confidence that God saw it fit to allow me to counsel, encourage, and offer solutions to some relationships' misfortune. Every praise is to God alone. Thank You, Lord.

I am grateful for my son, Anile Headley, for all his input, wisdom, and scriptures. I am so glad you are in my life.

I am also grateful for my son, Nashon Headley, for willingly contributing and discussing relevant issues affecting young people.

Gratitude goes out to all the youth who entrusted me with their personal issues. Thanks for sharing. Be guided by the wonderful narratives.

I humbly love and respect those adults who were never afraid to share with me their many marital downfalls. You are a hero.

Thanks to Pastor Denise Garwood for your constant prayers and positive feedback. It carried me a long way.

Thanks to Rachel Smith for her input and suggestions.

Countless thanks and appreciation to Joy Ehrenzweig for her dedication to prayer.

Thanks to Written Word Publishing LLC for the awesome work of refining and publishing this great book, *Swine and Pearls*.

*"Do not give what is holy
to the dogs; nor cast your
pearls before swine, lest
they trample them under
their feet, and turn and
tear you in pieces"*
(Matthew 7:6 NKJV).

Introduction

Swine and pearls are dissimilar to each other. They're a thought provoking and captivating way to draw your attention to how flippantly relationships are taken in our society. The words "swine and pearls" are used metaphorically to indicate features deeply rooted in this mundane world that have necessitated deep reflection and a switch in mindset. When you think about swine and pearls, what is the first thing that comes to mind? A group of pigs and an array of precious stones, right? Well, you are not far from the point. Only the context of using both words relate to love, your belief system and whom you deemed yourself to be.

Many things have indeed changed in the world that we live in. There is so much hate and self-conceitedness right now, and it has become uneasy for people to trust and love without fear. However, let's take a step back for a moment and approach this realism from God's perspective. He addresses this very issue in 1 John 4:18. He says there is no fear in love, but perfect love cast out all fear and he who fears is not made perfect in Christ. Note: true love stems from our perfect love for God. When we love God, we will also love our neighbors. There is a contrast between those who are rooted in the mundane of society and those who are grounded in God. Daily, we are exposed to plenty of content on broken marriages and the effect of damaging relationships. There is so much immorality in the world that many have begun to believe in the pessimistic idea that there is no such thing as true love anymore. As children of God, we must combat this ruthless artificial insemination created by society.

With the vast decline in the rate at which people believe in true love, the real question is, how many people go into real-time relationships because they are selflessly involved with their partners? Even when people say that they love their partners, in most instances, it is all because of a motive known or unknown to either party. Many people have derailed the true definition of love as a feeling of mutual cosmic connection imbued in us through the nature of God. Therefore, the Bible explains that we cannot claim to love if we do not know God, for God is love.

This impeccable narrative on swine and pearls is a mind cleanser. It reminds you there is a need to shift sides from conformity with what is in vogue in society and embrace our divine mandate. Each page of this book will teach you about the quintessential of loving and being invested in those you claim to love for the right reasons. As an adult, you must understand that your choices today will impact your life tomorrow. They might not affect you right now, but in the long run, the effects of your preferences determine the quality of life you will have. Although you may have made many mistakes in the past, it is never too late to start living the right way!

> Lord, today means everything to You. You are not here to condemn anyone. You are here to teach us wisdom. You are here to teach us that we can make wise choices even when we have made mistakes. You told us in Hebrews 3:15 (NKJV), *"Today, if you will hear His voice, Do not harden your heart as in the rebellion."* In Jesus' Name, Amen.

Today is the best time to turn around and heed God's counsel.

There are many things to learn from this fantastic read. First, you will discover a new definition of love. This new definition of love will drive you towards a sense of self-identification where you begin to mentally evaluate yourself, even as you make lifestyle changes that draw you to the love of God that defines your core. You will learn about the gems you have in your nature as a human that make you a pearl. This understanding will inspire you to make positive decisions about yourself and those you are intentional about.

A focal point that needs to be stated at this juncture is that so much about your life has been established in God's Word of truth. Investing time in the knowledge of God's Word as it pertains to your life will be the paradigm shift that changes your perception of love for the better. While reading through this spirit inspired narrative, you will learn about the dictates of God on dating, relationships, courtship, and features defining a long-lasting relationship that eventually leads to marriage.

The idea behind *Swine and Pearls* was laid in my mind a while back. The inspirational point for me has been my two young boys, growing and blossoming into teenagers, soon to become adults. If there is one fact I know to be accurate, it is that people who do not have a moral compass to follow when it comes to matters of the heart sometimes make life's greatest mistakes that could be avoided. I understand that lack of guidance is why the world has become the way it is. Over time, this change could include more voices like mine springing forth to talk about those things that many young ones are getting wrong.

For a society that seems so keen on education, one begins to wonder why there is a surge in the number of children born to parents out of wedlock. This goes to show that we are, in so many ways, lost. However, the problems we are dealing with now are nothing compared to what we would face if these current trends were not dealt with.

The plan of God for your life is that you flourish and do great exploits. Exploits will not always be financial. When you have a stable relationship meant to last a lifetime, you are said to be flourishing, just as God planned. While flipping through the pages of this book, understand the standard of God for your life is that you experience an abundance of joy and peace, which comes from knowing who you are in God's heart. Please do not give your pearls to swine; they will eternally damage your garment of honor.

Thanks.

The Power of the Mind

The mind is the most formidable dynamic of all humans. It can make you or break you. In Romans 12:2, the Scripture admonishes you to renew your mind daily to experience a total revolution which means you can become a new person in your thought man daily. It suddenly makes sense and has become more apparent why you must quickly deal with issues of the mind, including anger, and should not allow yourself to carry over issues to another day. As a matter of fact, in Ephesians 4:26, Paul tells you not to let the sun go down on your wrath.

The mind will be one of the most influential and valuable tools for a successful relationship. It can be extremely unruly at times; however, you must bring it under the subjection of the Holy Spirit. You can take every thought captive, especially if it's not in line with what God says. You must be conscious of the ideas that come to mind and circumvent them before they enter the heart.

Remember, what you think is crucial to who you are. If you are wondering how to prevent thoughts from coming to your mind, wonder no more. You can't stop them, but there is something you can do. Scripture reminds you that the weapon to fight the mind's thoughts must be approached from a spiritual angle. *"For the weapons of our warfare are not carnal, but mighty through God to the pulling down of strong holds"* (2 Corinthians 10:4).

Your mindset can cause the woes of your relationships and your life. This happens when you drift from the infallible Word of God and begin to lean on your own understanding, giving place to your self-destructive ego and pride. My heart aches to see how many marriages are dissolved in the most derogatory ways. This must be stopped with God's love. People must learn to let go of yesterday's pain and hurt. They must also learn to forgive one another.

Remember, you are not wrestling with flesh and blood but against principalities and powers whose only intentions are to destroy anything God stands for (Ephesians 6:12). Finally, arm yourself with the Word of God. It's your weapon and tool to help you stand. Having done all to stand, you are not a victim but a victor. You are expected to live the victorious life God promised you. When the thoughts of your mind test you, allow your mind to be tempered by the Holy Spirit. Your behavior tells how rooted you are in the Word of God. It is pride that will drive you to the conclusion that does not allow God to get the glory out of your life.

PART A
SELF-LOVE (INTRODUCTORY ASPECT)

CHAPTER ONE

Self-Love: A Pathway to Finding Your True Self

In Matthew 22:38-39, Jesus spoke about the importance of loving oneself. It is that kind of love you will give to the one you are seeking to find. He said, "You shall love your neighbor as yourself."

"Do not give what is holy to the dogs; nor cast your pearls before swine, lest they trample them under their feet, and turn and tear you into pieces" (Matthew 7:6 NKJV).

It is a strange sight to see at any point in time, pearls wrapped around the neck of swine. For context, a swine means a pig or a hog, which is affiliated with an unpleasant person, dirtiness and a special affection for mud. On the other hand, pearls indicate the carrier of precious stone, are unusually desirable and have a high quality, are defined as a gem, and have personal character. They are naturally perceived of others by the illumines light that radiates out of their appearance and naturally influences their social setting. To now find a pearl wrapped around a swine's neck would mean a lot of unpleasant speculations to the bystanders, and this is where the central theme of this chapter lies.

Although metaphorically utilized, there are clear distinctions between the character of a swine and a pearl. I am not just referring to the wearing of pearls but to be a replica of a pearl.

Some humans depict the characteristics of swine yet seek to have pearls around their neck. This conflicts with the lesson intended to be learned from this narrative. It means their personality does not align with a pearl's mentality or the individual they are seeking to be with, neither are they aligned with the attributes of Christ. This happens when, whether swine or pearl, there is a misplacement and a mismatch going on between two people. They did not carefully pay attention to red flags (the signs or warnings that are foretelling) in the initial stage of their relationship. Instead of breaking off, they overlook and continue until they find themselves in something that poses a more difficult challenge to pull out of. Sometimes, for various reasons, people go head-on and become blindfolded in their voyage of seeking love. It's safe to say one's feeling of attraction or infatuation overrides their standard in the dating process which was only meant to be a means for searching out. When they reach this point, it is necessary to make a list of what they're feeling before going on a date. They should question their motive and ask themselves, "What am I looking for?" Some reasons many individuals encounter relationship trouble are:

1. Their time clock is ticking away
2. All their friends are doing it
3. They feel the need to explore and experience
4. They are lonely
5. They get married so sex will not be a sin
6. A reason other than love

Feel free to make your own list which will help you to program the right mindset before dating. I encourage you to wait on God's timing. Don't let fear grab hold of you. Remember what His Words says in 2 Timothy 1:7, *"For God hath not given us the spirit of fear; but of power, and of love, and of a sound mind."* Henceforth, you are valuable and precious. Consequently, the investment of God in you is that of power, love and a sound mind. You carry special features that are gems which distinguish you from the world around you. It is impressive that the Bible reckons this side to your personality when it says in the Book of Psalm 139:14, *"I will praise thee; for I am fearful and wonderfully made."*

These three important virtues are crucial for defining the concept of self-love. Self-love stems from a place of self-respect. It means you should have high regard for yourself in such a way that you already set a standard for what is perfect and conducive for you. It is the ability to set a moral code for what is good and acceptable to you. The ability to love yourself unconditionally would prevent you from settling for things that undermine your love for yourself. Quite interestingly, many people say they love those with whom they have a close relationship. Most times, this is often said without understanding the love for self. Sadly, there is no way you can say you love others without practicing that same love on yourself first. This is because you cannot give what you do not have. These days, it is common to find people in toxic relationships. Nobody ever wakes up one morning and then decides to end up in a toxic relationship. However, because the love for self is lacking, it allows such humans to settle for whatever life presents to them.

Perhaps, one personality in the Bible that reminds us of the need to love oneself is the personality of Jesus Christ. This is our set standard anyway. During the earthly ministry of Jesus, He showed love to His disciples and all those He met. This great demonstration of loving others unconditionally speeds up a unique kind of acceptance of a life-changing transformation. When you can demonstrate to others that you care about them, you will win their love and trust that can last for a lifetime. 1 John 3:18 tells us that we should not only love in words or speech but in action and truth. Understand that true love takes hospitality, treating each other with kindness and respect. It plays a great role when you are looking for your life partner. Relationships come with lots of maturity and responsibilities.

However, rather than settling for the bandwagon (the society and common trends), Jesus' love for others made Him act differently. He always had something to offer others. Do not only set your mind on financial gifts. Look at the way

He communicated with those He encountered. One may argue that Jesus did not love Himself. They may or may not be right. It is noteworthy to interpreted or translate the behavior of Jesus. He simply demonstrated what true love is all about. One can conclude that Jesus was selfless even to the point of death.

This next statement is not intended to specify neither the husband nor the wife to be swine or pearl. However, for the point of conversation, Scripture says a husband should love his wife in such a way to the point of giving up his life for her, and in the same breath, a wife must submit herself to her husband (Ephesians 5:25-28). This command defines how a perfect love relationship should be.

As a human with inner pearls (character) that make you a gem in the world, you should not be found settling for what others do. Remember, you have a set of guidelines to operate under. You are a right-thinking human and there are times when you might be tempted to act out of character. This is when you must be intentionally aware of who you are. However, you do not have to settle for certain things because it is the practice in society. Just because it is good for others does not mean it is proper for you. This is why it is trite to identify ways by which you can imbue self-love into your daily life.

Ways to Imbue Self-Love into Your Daily Life

- **Do Unto Yourself That Which You Would Want Others to Do to You:** It is often said that one should do unto others what one would want others to do to oneself. This is from the perspective of retributive justice. However, in self-love, the standard is to do to yourself what you want others to do to you. This is quite important because it teaches you how to balance the love you give others and how much love can be reciprocated. There is no excess giving out of love. By doing to yourself that you would want others to do to you, you set a standard of expectation for yourself. In the end, this allows you to mentally evaluate yourself and refrain from settling for any kind of love.

    Understanding how you treat yourself would give you an idea of how you want to be loved. In this case, just any kind of love is not good enough for you because there is a standard that you have already set for yourself.

- **Don't Put Yourself in a Place of Self-Sabotage:** One of the many indicative ways to know that you lack the love for self is when you are invested in the continuous act of self-sabotage. What self-sabotaging means here is that you constantly have that mindset of not being good enough. This prevents you from having a mind of your own and deciding to do what you have always planned to do. Your ideas do not validate your actions if you are constantly in this mindset. External forces would. Hence, every time you act on something, you are doing it because someone outside your mind validated it. This is anti-self-love because it means you do not have a mind of your own.

  Self-love does not mean you are not mentally aware of your flaws and weaknesses. Regardless of those flaws, you are still a valid and relevant person. Recall the story of Moses in the Bible. Moses was a stutterer, but the mandate of God for his life was that he would be the one to lead the children of Israel out of Egypt. He was on the verge of self-sabotage because of his stuttering trait. However, he was reminded of his purpose to the children of

Israel and his need to love himself for who he was.

One way to stop self-sabotage is to have a sense of purpose or a goal. When you do so, you will, by default, learn to love yourself, which affects how you treat yourself.

- **Never Compromise Your Moral Codes:** In case you do not know, your moral codes are things you consider to be right or wrong. They form a core part of who you are. Moral codes can vary from person to person depending on what you accept as right or wrong. If you have to compromise your moral codes from time to time, then it means you do not love yourself enough and your moral code is shaky.

"This book of the law shall not depart out of thy mouth; but thou shall meditate therein day and night, that thou mayest observe to do according to all that is written therein: for then thou shalt make thy way prosperous, and then thou shalt have good success"
(Joshua 1:8).

Your moral codes are your personal law, rules, and regulation you live by. If there is one thing that you should learn from Joshua 1:8, it is that the only way that you can enhance the quality of your life and attain the sort of success as never before is to diligently observe to do those things that form your moral codes. When you always compromise your moral codes, you go below the bar, which spells defeat.

Note: Self-love is all about understanding yourself and who you are. It is the ability to mentally evaluate your standards from time to time to redefine who you are and those that you are seeking to have a relationship with.

CHAPTER TWO

Self-Identification and How It Is a Vital Trait for Quality Decision Making

"to know the love of Christ which passes knowledge; that you may be filled with all the fullness of God"
(Ephesians 3:19 NJKV).

Self-identification means the ability of a person to understand and state, factually, who they are. Self-identification stems from a place of self-knowledge. It means you are aware of so much information about yourself that you can say you are either good or bad. If ten people were arranged in a room and asked to identify if they are a worthy fit for a leadership role within an organization, it is most probable that all ten would say they are worthy. The reason for this is, as humans, we are triggered to live in denial of who we are. The logical explanation is we want to look good in the eyes of others.

Self-identification requires the ability to assess yourself from a personal point of view in opposed to the point of view that intends to impress others. It is the ability to evaluate yourself based on your personality traits to state the kind of person you are. When you can assess the kind of person you are, it becomes easier to navigate your assessment to find the kind of partner that is most in sync with you.

A lot of things have gone wrong in today's world. When a lot of young ones intend to relate to the reason why they love their partner, many are driven to talk about attraction, beauty and other commendable adjectives that can only work for a short time. When it comes to having a partner with whom you intend to spend the rest of your life, your most prized asset would be to select someone who perfectly syncs with you. You will only be able to find this kind of person when you have identified yourself based on your traits and characteristics. Now, let's explore ways by which you can self-identify.

How to Utilize Self-Identification for the Purpose of Making Quality Decisions When Choosing Your Partner

- **Ask Yourself the Question, "Who Am I?"** A wise man once said that one of the most difficult questions humans seldom answer is, "Who am I?" The reason is that humans, by their very nature, prefer to live in denial of themselves. They prefer to live in abeyance with what looks and sounds appealing to the ears of others. At the end of the day, the ability to understand who you are and act in tandem with what you know about yourself would go a long way in helping to identify and accept yourself. Believe it or not, you can only accept who you are when you identify with your character traits.

  In order to put facts into context, based on your assessment of yourself, if you find out that you are more of an introvert, it might be more appealing to select an extrovert for a life partner. This is so they will complement the very reserved aspect of your life. Although this is not a standard, it could be a consideration point.

  Answering the question *"Who am I?"* might sometimes require that you make use of a S.W.O.T analysis table. This table is divided into four segments: *Strengths, Weaknesses, Opportunities, and Threats.* Segmenting your traits into all four aspects of the S.W.O.T. table would help you evaluate your personality and come to an acceptance of who you are. When you have been able to itemize your strengths, weaknesses, opportunities, and threats, you will understand what you need to work on and those things you need to let go of to find the partner you seek.

Conversely, while you are trying to answer the question *"Who am I,"* it is also imperative to have it at the back of your mind that the kind of partner you seek will also have expectations of you. It is the mere reason why Amos 3:3 says, *"Can two walk together, except they be agreed?"* The answer is, **no**! This is why when you are charting a pathway towards answering the question *"Who am I,"* you must keep in mind that the reason for this question is to make yourself a worthy standard for your prospective partner.

• **What Standards are You Setting in Place to Find the One You Seek?** There is a common saying, where there is no law, there is no sin. Earlier, I mentioned setting a standard for yourself regarding self-love. However, when it comes to finding a partner you intend to spend the rest of your life with, you will also need to set a standard of expectations. A lot of people set improper standards for the one they seek because they base their standard of expectations on vanities. By vanities, I mean the things you can see with your eyes or the things that can be overlooked in a wider scheme of events. Many young ones look amiss when setting standards for their partners, and this is where they get it wrong. Setting standards amiss is why many young women today will describe attributes they want in a man such as white or black, light skin or dark skin, tall, and handsome. They say these things so casually as though these are the most important things to focus on when choosing a life partner. Your guidelines are the foundation upon which your relationship with your future mate rests. When the foundation is destroyed, what can the righteous do?

Talking about standards set in place for the one you seek, the story of Esther comes to mind. In the Book of Esther chapter 2, the Bible records that Esther was pliant, obedient, and virtuous. A juxtapose of these virtues is what the King saw that made him choose her as his wife. There were other women in the palace, but the standard he had already set for himself made him choose Esther as his Queen. Standards allow you to know the yardstick for selecting a life partner.

Setting standards for the one you seek sometimes depends on how you see yourself. For instance, if you are Christian, to have sanctity and orderliness in your relationship, it makes a lot of sense to get married to one who is also a Christian. This way, your belief systems and moral codes would not be up for debate. The essence of setting standards for the one you seek is clearly defining the relationship you want with your chosen partner. It helps to make things easier.

- **Who are You Looking For?** When looking for a life partner, you need to understand whom you are looking for. The answer to this question would depend solely on your lifestyle and values. Selecting a life partner means choosing someone who can handle the technicalities of setting up a home. This would include cohabitation, children, and family life amongst others. Your lifestyle and values must be high on the priority list and any other important factors should be considered when seeking your life partner.

There are a lot of broken homes today. Most times, in divorce court, so much is said about the wrongs that a party has done or how incompatible the two parties are. However, if the spouses had been able to decipher what they were looking for before they began the relationship, things would have been more substantial. When you understand the kind of person you are looking for, you have an idea of the threshold you are willing to accommodate because your partner fits into your description. This helps you both avoid a lot of drama years into the relationship.

- **Where Do You Expect to Find Your Life Partner?** Where you find a person, directly or remotely, speaks volumes about their preferences. We live in an age where people love to go to clubs and attend parties. If you meet a person at a party, it shows you firsthand that they can be social. Whether they like to attend parties every other day is what you would likely find out later. However, an important point has been highlighted, and it is that they like to attend parties.

It is easier to adjudge someone whom you would love to become your life partner when you can almost predict what they would be

25

doing at every time of the day. This is the basis upon which many marriage counsellors would admonish intending lovers to become friends before they delve into a relationship. Predictability is a virtue when selecting a life's friend, partner, lover and shouldn't be treated with laxity.

Everyone needs friends but choosing friends must be intentional because they can play a significant role in your life. There are many qualities to look for in potential friends. Some great benefits from good friendships are encouragement, accountability, and companionship, just to name a few.

You must be careful with who you form bonds with. Avoid friends who are toxic and energy draining. Think about what's meaningful and important to you and what would be considered detrimental to your life, then make a list of what traits you would look for in a friend. One remarkable asset to look for is someone who will love and stand with you through thick and thin. The Scripture states, *"A friend loveth at all times"* (Proverbs 17:17). Always seek individuals who are reliable and full of wisdom. It will help you to become wiser because you can learn from them or perhaps follow in their footsteps. If your friends are productive, you will also be productive.

Look above the natural meaning of their career, possessions and outward appearance. As you get closer to someone, you will get a better understanding of what is on the inside. See if they possess the fruit of the spirit–love, joy, peace, forbearance, kindness, goodness, faithfulness, gentleness, and self-control. Pursuing anyone trying to find out their tendencies should lead to an admirable outcome. In other words, do not waste your time if someone is unproductive, negative, full of anger, and the opposite of the fruit of the Spirit. My advice to you is to make sure you already possess the characteristics you are looking for so they can be mirrored in the person with whom you are seeking to pursue a relationship.

A true friend can help guide your way to happiness and fulfilment. It is always best to seek a friend before you need one. It is adorable if you bond with a friend who eventually becomes your pearl. Strive to build a healthy friendly relationship with that special someone and let that friendship continue to grow even through your marriage, this way you will become one as it was intended to be.

Make a list of what's important in the kind of friendship you are seeking:

1. _____

2. _____

3. _____

4. _____

5. _____

6. _____

CHAPTER THREE

Self-Relationship and How It Affects Your Interpersonal Life with Others

"This is the first and greatest commandment. And the second is like it: 'You shall love your neighbor as yourself'" (Matthew 22:37-39).

Self-relationship is an offshoot of self-love. The Bible records that the nature of God is love. It would also be recalled that a further exposition about the ten commandments shows that love is the greatest commandment of all. The Bible went on to emphasize the love of your neighbors as yourself. Also, as highlighted earlier, you cannot give what you do not have. It is on this basis that you need to love yourself first. When you love yourself, it becomes easier to have a relationship with yourself.

As a human, you are a product of the things that you have experienced over time. However, you must imbue the ability to have a relationship with yourself. The reason is that self-relationship stems from a place of acceptance—an acceptance of those things that you cannot change, an acceptance of your experiences, an acceptance of your healing after you might have been hurt, and other forms of acceptance that are healthy for your mind frame. You need to understand that who you will be when you have a relationship with a life partner depends on how you treat yourself. If you are the kind of person who finds it hard to forgive yourself for a wrong that you did to someone else unknowingly, it means you do not have the maturity to forgive others and let things go. This rubs off on people when you are in a relationship and they wrong you.

Self-relationship allows you to see yourself for whom you are, and it allows you to accept your strengths and weaknesses as you journey through life. Sometimes, you find people who do not have a manner of approach with those within their social settings. Such kinds of people are sometimes viewed as insensitive, but this is not always the case. As a matter of fact, it could be because they do not have a relationship with themselves. Self-relationship allows you to evaluate things that are good for you and keeps you in check about how to interact with those within your social space.

One crucial way to know if you have a healthy self-relationship is if you have a mind that communicates with your being. The quality of the conversations you have with yourself determines whether you have a healthy self-relationship or not. This is why the Book of Proverbs 23:7 says that as a man thinketh in his heart, so is he. Your thoughts determine the kind of relationship you have with yourself. When you have a healthy relationship with yourself, it is easier to say that you are a good person earlier than others.

At times, you may undervalue the place of conversations that you can have with yourself. There are times when you might plan to act irrationally, but a second thought in you prevents it. This is because you have a healthy relationship with yourself. A healthy relationship with yourself stems from understanding God's standard in your life.

You would recall the biblical story of King Saul. The Bible records that after he had disobeyed the commandment of God, the Spirit of God left him and the evil spirit entered him. He began to act incoherently afterwards. This means that the ability to have a healthy relationship with yourself is premised on your understanding of the kind of love that God expects you to have. It is what defines your moral values and how you interact with others.

There are a lot of benefits to relating effectively with yourself. A fundamental benefit is finding yourself and defining who you are. In many social contexts, it is usually said that one cannot be a judge in their own case. While this is a valid point, self-relationship allows you to adjudicate yourself before others begin to evaluate your personality based on how you interact with them. For instance, relating with yourself will allow you to know if you have a narcissistic tendency or are naturally selfish. Understanding that you have these tendencies shows that you are flawed. This understanding triggers you to find a way to take out that flaw so you can be a better person to your loved one and those with whom you have any form of relationship.

Here are a few nuggets to bear in mind should you decide you want to live a life that thrives on a self-relationship:

1. **Be Intentional and Mentally Aware of Whom You Are:** As a human, you may often

be advised to define the kind of relationship you have with people within your social setting. This is because it allows you to define a goal for the kind of relationship you have with those people. For instance, when you are emotionally attracted to someone, it is best to define such a relationship with the other person because you both understand. It becomes easier to navigate a pathway to a sustainable relationship.

Bringing this understanding into the realm of self-relationship, you must understand the aim of trying to strike a relationship with yourself. This will allow you to evaluate the kind of person you are. When you have been able to mentally evaluate yourself, you can decide if you are ready for the sort of relationship you intend to have with your future life partner.

This brings to mind the story of King David and Bathsheba in 2 Samuel 11 and 12. King David had already sinned against God by sleeping with Bathsheba and killing her husband. God then sent Prophet Nathan to tell him a story in the form of a parable. This was the tale of the rich man with many sheep and the poor man with just one. The rich man took the only sheep the poor man had. After hearing the story, King David realized his wrong and he entered a realm of what is now known as godly sorrow. He was remorseful and had to take some time off to reevaluate himself and rekindle the love of God that had been sent down on us as humans.

An important lesson that can be taken from King David's story is that when one has not imbued the habit of relating with self, they act based on selfish thoughts, experiences and positions in life. At that point, they have mastered the art of self-relationship and ultimately react like David. They have this personal sense of godly sorrow, and it triggers them to want to expunge themselves from those things that make them act short of the better person they are supposed to be.

2. **Set Your Self-Relationship Journey on a Pedestal of Goals You Intend to Achieve:** If there is one thing that is clear about life generally, it is that short term gratifications keep your fire burning. Imagine that feeling when you got your first job. There was a drive in you to go to work daily. Why? Because you were certain that by the end of the week or month, you would receive a set wage. However, after a long period, the energy began

to drop because you had seen this play out too much, and maybe your craving for life had become more intense. You realized that you were not as interested in your job as when you started. To maintain the drive that would keep you going to that workplace, the gratification system would have to change from just earning to other things you enjoy. It is exactly the same with self-relationship.

Your self-relationship journey, after finding out some of the traits you intend to change, should focus on a reward system for changing those traits. It could be within a one- or two-month time frame. A while after that, you must graduate from a short-term reward system to a gratification system that ensures you do not let go of the new habits you have imbued in yourself.

3. **Be Anxious About the Change You Seek, But Give It Time:** There is a common saying that time heals everything. However, not much is said about the acceptance of time. Frequently, individuals are so engrossed in the need to see the change they seek so much that they begin to get impatient when the change does not come quickly. A rule of thumb you should know about unbreaking some habits

with yourself is the change you seek might not become a part of you immediately; you need to give yourself some time. Accepting that things change with time is the only way you would appreciate your self-relationship journey.

Note: One of the ways you can evaluate your self-relationship journey is to be very conscious about yourself and identify when you have been able to teach yourself to see the good in others. Imagine Jesus Christ during His earthly ministry. He could do well everywhere He went because there was a consciousness of who He was. It is that consciousness that led Him to see the good in others and gave Him a reason to create positive change during His time on earth.

While self-relationship is about making yourself a better person, its manifestation can only be seen from an outward perspective. A typical example is how you treat others.

CHAPTER FOUR

A Purpose Driven Mind as a Yardstick for Reaching Your Goals and Living a Better Life

"Declaring the end from the beginning, And from ancient times things that are not yet done, Saying, 'My counsel shall stand, And I will do all My pleasure,"
(Isaiah 46:10 NKJV).

There is so much about your life as a human that tells a story of the kind of mindset you have. Whether you like it or not, you are a product of the kind of mind you carry. When one has a dirty mind, they will often wonder why they cannot have a perfect life; but a dirty or immoral mind leads the way to a messy and immoral life. That is the rule of life, and it is how the universe responds to the emitted energy. It is no wonder the Bible said in the Book of Matthew 12:34 that the mouth speaks out of the abundance of the heart. The connotative meaning in today's world is that the kind of mind one has will determine what their reality will be. This is why one of the goals of self-awareness for anyone who intends to change the course of their life is to become sensitive about their mind.

A purpose driven mindset is a mindset that stems from the idea that one desires to grow. What a lot of people do not know is growth in life can be very divergent. When you have a purpose driven mindset, all your ideation of things would be geared towards ensuring you attain the growth you so keenly seek. Bringing this into the context of this discussion, a purpose driven mindset regarding finding a partner means you are willing to do all it takes to ensure the relationship with your other half works out. Why is this fundamental? It is fundamental because there would be circumstances that militate against the relationship you have with your other half. The sense of purpose and the zest to make things work out inspires you to keep the fire of your love burning.

Today's world thrives on many misconstrued realities. If you start a discussion in a big hall about finding love and staying true to your partner, you will find many speakers declaring that love is about sweet and blissful experiences. You would seldom find speakers talking about how love can always have its own rock bottom. The truth is love wouldn't always be as you expect it to be. This is because you and your partner are two different entities who have made up your minds to make things work. This is why compromises have to be made sometimes. However, it is not only the compromises that make relationships work; having a purpose driven mindset also works.

A narrative that perhaps draws this point close to home is the relationship of God with us as humans. By our mundane human standards, we are not worthy or qualified for the kind of love God gives us, yet He loves us. If you have a relationship with your partner where you both quarrel and constantly have an urge to break up, it is because one or both of you lacks a purpose driven mindset. It means the foundation of the relationship was not built on the desire to grow or build the kind of love that stands the test of time, and if the foundation is destroyed, what can the righteous do?

Finding purpose in the relationship you have right now should, first of all, start with you. You have to be able to define the kind of relationship you have with your partner. What is your plan for the relationship? Is it because you just enjoy their company, or do you love them so much you cannot imagine living a *happily ever after life* without them? Many people go into a relationship without the ability to define their relationship. Before you kickstart a working relationship, you must first have envisaged in your mind what it should seem like. This ideation of things gives you the conviction you should proceed with. This foundation also gives your supposed relationship a sense of purpose. When you have found the purpose for which your relationship should start, you will be able to plan with your partner those goals that make your love wax stronger.

Communication with your partner is another way by which you show there is a purpose for the relationship to thrive. Sadly, a lot of people have misconceptions about communication. Yes, it is said that for communication to be complete, the decoder has to understand the encoder. However, in love ties and building working relationships, communication means you understand the tonality with which your partner loves to be communicated. This is where the idea of love languages comes into context. For some people, their love language might be gifts. For others, their love language may be words of validation or affirmation. For this reason, communicating in love terms means you are observant enough to know and understand the way your partner would love to be communicated with, and you must be more than willing to do so.

According to the words of Gary Chapman, "the secret to the sort of love that lasts long is to understand your partner's love language." There are a lot of ways to know your partner's love language. Being observant will reveal how they respond to certain acts done in love. If you both communicate effectively, it is easier to express your love languages.

Ways to Develop a Purpose Driven Mindset in a Relationship

1. **Effectively Communicating About Values:** Earlier, I mentioned the need to communicate effectively in a relationship. This is so you both would be on the same page, especially as it relates to those things that keep the fire of your love burning. One thing that should be communicated is the values which define your relationship. All humans have a personal sense of value, but every relationship has to stand for something. However, it becomes hard to wax

stronger in love if you don't come to terms with your relationship's values.

Communicating what you both would want the relationship to stand for would go a long way in defining your relationship. This way, it becomes much easier to disagree and then agree on what works. Having a purpose driven mindset in your relationship is more about intentionality. Sometimes, there is no way for your partner to understand how intentional you are about the relationship if you do not communicate effectively with each other.

There is a common saying that there is no sin when there is no law. Those communicated and agreed upon values are like the laws upon which your relationship sails. You should both agree on those things that should not be done while you are on this dating journey. Have you ever met a couple and it appeared that talking to one felt almost like you were talking to the other half? Their answers to questions were so much in sync that you could almost predict what one or the other would say? This is what effective communication of values does to your relationship. You both become so intertwined that your world rubs off on that of your partner.

2. **Making Daily Connection with Your Partner:** An African proverb says there is no way that the lizard will come into your home except for a crack in the wall. In a relationship, you must understand that you have different temperaments and moods. What this means is, the way you both cope with situations would differ a great deal. There will be times when your partner does not feel like communicating. In those times, they need you to try to understand them. There are a ton of reasons why this could be the case. It might be because of emotions from the past, and they need your strength at that point to carry on. Making second guesses and being insecure would only kill the vibe that should revolve around your relationship.

This brings to mind a salient point that is sometimes made about the 80/20 rule. What the 80/20 rule admonishes as it relates to love is there is no such thing as a relationship that is 100 percent perfect. On some days, your partner would give you 20 percent of their energy. In those moments, they expect you to complement their effort with 80 percent of your energy. On other days, as there would always be, you would also crave 80 percent of your partner's energy because you would only be able to give 20 percent of yours. I am trying to say that a purpose driven mindset would help you build a connection that works with your partner. There would be no reason to separate or break apart because your connection has become the force upon which your relationship wax strengthens.

PART B
FINDING YOUR PERFECT PEARLS: BUILDING A HEALTHY RELATIONSHIP IN A GODLY MANNER

CHAPTER FIVE

Building True Love on the Foundation of God's Words

"There is no fear in love; but perfect love casts out fear, because fear involves torment. But he who fears has not been made perfect in love" (1 John 4:18).

In the Book of Matthew 7:25-27, our mind was drawn quickly to two different kinds of buildings. The one that was built on a sandy foundation, and when the rain poured, the house fell greatly. On the other hand, a house was built on a rock. When the rain fell on that house, the house didn't fall. Why? Because the foundation was solid. This analogy could also relate immensely to the context of building true love. It would be recalled that the Bible records the greatest of all commandments is love. However, from an etymological standpoint, there are variants to love, but the greatest of them all starts with the love of God. You cannot claim to be building true love with your partner if you do not love God. This is what many who are in the world do not realize. It is easy to say you are in love with a person, but from what kind of mindset do you say this? This says a lot about who you are or the kind of relationship you are likely to have.

The ten commandments give us an insight into the kind of mind God expects us to have. A mindset that does not thrive on sin. Otherwise, why would the commandments talk about such things as thou shall not kill and thou shall not convert thy neighbor's property? It is because there is a standard of expectations when we say we are one with God. All of this makes a lot of sense now, given that we live in a world where sex and immorality have become the order of the day. People now have a misconceived perception of love. Love to so many young ones doesn't have a standard. It involves sex and frolicking around, all of which are against the standard God has set for us as Christians or lovers of the world.

An assessment of your relationship with your loved one would make you understand what kind of relationship you will share with your spouse. As the text of this chapter dictates, if the kind of love you have for your partner makes you feel scared and insecure, something is wrong. The kind of love that God has for us does not accept fear. God was not insecure about what we would become or whether we would accept the faith through Christ when He sent His son to die for our sins. The godly kind of love should give you assurance and not cause you to harbor iniquity. Illicit sex, lack of trust and anger do not represent the godly kind of love.

When trying to build a godly kind of relationship with your partner, the Bible verse that should ring in your mind is the Book of Mark 12:30 which says, *"And thou shalt love the Lord thy God with all thy heart, and with all thy soul, and with all thy mind, and with all thy strength."* Interestingly, this chapter of the Bible shows you how to love your partner. The standard of love you should have towards your partner should allow you to love them with all your being. When you love someone

47

with the core of everything that makes you who you are, there would be no room for second guesses, which is what the Word of God shows us about building true love.

Also, the Book of Matthew 5:16 says, *"that they may see your good works and glorify your Father which is in heaven."* The pattern of the godly kind of relationship should showcase more of how much you love God. On this basis, when people see and experience the love you share with your partner, they can see the personality of God manifesting through your relationship. It is why the Bible says that they would see the good works of God in you and glorify God through you. When your relationship with your loved one is built on the Word of God, you realize that your life pattern becomes a standard for which people want to define their relationship. This is void of lust or any earthly affinity, built on the core values under which your relationship with your partner is defined.

The Book of Matthew 22:39 also preaches another standard in God's Word about love for your partner. It says, "love your neighbour as thyself." This means you should love your partner just as much as you would love yourself. As a normal human, you are bound to love yourself enough not to put yourself in harm's way. The Bible verse also admonishes that you should endeavor to love your partner as much as you love yourself. It is on this platform that you end up loving them relentlessly, regardless of how flawed they might be.

Ways to Inculcate the Word of God into Your Conception of True Love

1. **Love with Integrity:** One of the reasons relationships today don't last too long is that the foundation of most mundane relationships is built on ulterior motives and deceit. This is regardless of how much couples claim to love themselves. In today's world, young ladies find themselves getting married to men because of vanities—money, sex and trying to get involved with men who would take them out of their predicaments. At the end of the day, when the vanities they seek halt, they find no reason to continue with the acclaimed relationship because the foundation upon which the relationship was built was on ulterior motives.

   The Bible admonishes us to love God in spirit and in truth. Drawing a linkage from this portion of the Bible into your relationship should show you that the attitude of God towards the love for your partner should be premised on truth and not on other motives that one might have as a mundane human. The Book of Ephesians 4:25 admonished with keen interest on this when it said, *"Wherefore putting away lying, speak every man truth with his neighbour; for we are members one of another."* Hence, you should endeavor to love your partner in truth because you both share a bond that makes you a part of each other.

While you might feel that the basis for which you should love your partner is because of the goal of living happily ever after, the Bible also records in Proverbs 29:5 that when you indulge in a relationship with your partner based on lies and flattery, you indirectly spread a net around your feet. Hence, the karmic verdict of the universe giving back to you based on the pattern of love you show towards your partner is also inferred.

2. **Loving without Condition:** If there is anything that can be learned from the personality of God, it is that God loves unconditionally. Imagine a situation where God loves you with an ulterior motive in mind.

There would be no need to send His Son to come to die for the sins of humans.

As opposed to the personality of God, in today's world, most of the love people say they have for their partners are premised on conditions. This manifests how married men find it hard to show off their wives in public. When asked why this is the case, their most likely response would be they are private people who feel their love life should be kept on a low profile. Sadly, the Word of God admonishes showing off one's partner. The reason is that as much as your love life might be between you and your partner, the bulk of the trials you would face due to your relationship are based on external factors.

Thinking about love without conditions, the story that comes to mind is Jonathan's love for David. There were more than enough reasons to hide his love for his friend because showing off was more of a threat to him than his friend. However, because his love for David was without borders, he made himself vulnerable. At the end of the day, they were both better because of it.

In contrast, when Abraham denied Sarah as his wife, they faced a myriad of troubles. But for the love that God had for Abraham, there is a possibility that he might have lost his wife on the pedestal of keeping things private. This is why the love for our partners that the Word of God admonishes is the sort that is not shy to be disclosed in public. All the more reason why we love God privately, but God wants us to spread the gospel of truth so that more people can see and attest to His love for mankind.

3. **The Attribute of Mutual Edification and Growing in the Knowledge of His Truth:** The Bible cautions us not to be unequally yoked with sinners. The standard this gives to your love tie is that you should endeavor to build a relationship with people who share a mutual moral code with you. When you build a relationship with someone who is in the Christian faith, you are certain that irrespective of their denomination, the moral standard of truth for you both is the salvation that Jesus Christ has to offer. Whatever variation in a belief system might exist after that is secondary and can be redefined.

   When you build a relationship with someone in the Christian faith, it becomes easier to navigate the pathway of that relationship. You both can decide on what works for your relationship based on the knowledge of God's truth that you both are aware of. There is a reason that mundane relationships differ from God's defined relationship. This is because of the void of knowledge of God's Word. It is the reason why people who build their relationships without the knowledge of God's Word hold grudges for a very long time. They harbor so much anger in them that it becomes too hard to continue with the relationship after a while.

Apart from love and relationships, there are salient virtues for an interpersonal relationship that one can get from knowing God's truth. They are all embedded in the nine fruits of the Spirit. These virtues would help to inculcate a better lifestyle with others, which, in turn, rubs off on your relationship with your partner. The fruits of the Spirit are love, joy, peace, longsuffering, gentleness, goodness, faith, meekness, and temperance (Galatians 5:22-23).

4. **The Altruistic Perspective:** If there is one thing you should naturally learn about human nature, it is that by default, humans are selfish beings who, most times, seek their personal interests ahead of that of others. However, this

is not the admonition of God's Word. When building a true love relationship with your partner based on God's Word, the standard that God proclaims is exemplified in the Book of Matthew 7:12 (NKJV), *"Therefore, whatever you want men to do to you, do also to them."* This book is more or less an offshoot of what we all know as the golden rule. However, the difference is that you need to consider your partner's interest as much as you consider yours. This is because their interest is as important as yours. Making your partner feel that their interests and cravings matter is one of the many ways to boost your relationship, and it also adheres to the Word of God.

Note: The basis of building a relationship based on the Word of God is to build an edifying relationship premised on faith in God. There is a need to emphasize that God also admonishes the love of one's neighbor. Hence, all of the virtues you might learn from the Word of God should not be utilized only in the relationship with your partner. It should also be exercised in your interaction with other humans, irrespective of the value that they offer to you.

The standard of the Bible is clear about interpersonal relationships. If you do not love your fellow human whom you see daily, then it would be harder to love God, whom you have not seen but feel His impact.

CHAPTER SIX

Distinguishing Unconditional Love from Worldy Lust

"…above all things have fervent love for one another, for 'love will cover a multitude of sins'"
(1 Peter 4:8 NKJV).

There is a need to discuss the difference between unconditional love and worldly lust to appreciate the pearls in you. It is this variation of things that many people do not understand, and this explains why there are many broken marriages in the world today. It is because so many people have a wrong interpretation of their love towards their respective spouses that it has become hard for people to cope with each other. A valid point to make at this juncture is unconditional love stems from the divine, and it is different from the worldly lust which is known to man. While unconditional love is premised on the love for others as oneself. Worldly lust is selfish and does not consider the interest of others.

The Bible gives a better purview of the distinction between unconditional love and worldly lust in the Book of 2 Timothy 3:2-7, *"For men shall be lovers of their own selves, covetous, boasters, proud, blasphemers, disobedient to parents, unthankful, unholy, Without natural affection, trucebreakers, false accusers, incontinent...For of this sort are they which creep into houses, and lead captive silly women laden with sins, led away with diverse lusts, Ever learning, and never able to come to the knowledge of the truth."* In essence, what this Scripture is trying to explain is that the nature of worldly lust deals with all of those features that embrace the works of the flesh (sin). Worldly lust is against the perfection through Christ Jesus that God, through the Bible, declares.

As opposed to the unconditional love that one needs to have with their partner, worldly lust is a feeling that stems from satisfying the urge of the body. It could be lust based on a sex drive towards someone, lust for power, or any other variant. Typically, the way it operates is you begin to allow the lustful feeling to control you. This is why there are men who are so power drunk that they can go as far as killing someone just to ensure they get the control they seek. There are also women who, in turn for benefits, give their bodies. When you realize you have that constant need to satisfy a bodily craving, it's likely you are lustful.

In discussing worldly lust, the Book of Matthew 5:28 (NKJV) says, *"But I say to you that whoever looks at a woman to lust for her has already committed adultery with her in his heart."* Lustful acts, just like all other actions, start from the mind. The Bible says that at the very point when you have begun to nurture a lustful idea in your heart, you have sinned.

Interestingly, the unconditional love God expects you to have towards your partner is different from worldly love. People describe worldly love as a feeling that triggers your attraction towards your partner. However, in the context of the Word of God, unconditional love was defined in the Book of 1 Corinthians 13:4-7 (NKJV) as *"long and is kind; love does not envy; love does not parade itself, is not puffed up; does not behave rudely, does not seek its own, is not provoked, thinks no evil; does not rejoice in iniquity, but rejoices in the truth; bears all things, believes all things, hopes all things, endures all things."* All these features represent how you should practice unconditional love with your partner. The one that interests me the most is that love rejoices in the truth. That portion of the verse reveals so many details about the other features. You would find that if you are not the kind of person who loves their partner in truth, it becomes extremely hard to practice all the other features of unconditional love.

Remarkably, many people, even Christians, believe unconditional love cannot be practiced between lovers. This is because they have this myopic ideation of unconditional love being the sort that existed between David and Jonathan. Well, while they might be right to an extent, it would be proper to state here that in order for you to say that you truly love your partner, you must first consider them your friend. When you consider someone your friend, it is hard to become selfish with them because you love them just as much as you love yourself. On this pedestal, you find that you can be patient with them, you do not rejoice when they are doing things wrong, and you certainly would not be arrogant in your display of love towards them.

In today's world, many people love their partners, but they are also quick to rub it in their faces when they have constantly done a favor for them. Love is not arrogant and pride, and this is why when you love someone truly, from the depth of your heart, you would never be able to respond to them in this manner.

Sadly, a lot is not said about lust nowadays. Why? It has become a standard of acceptance in a world where people hate to hear the truth. Lustful actions have become people's reality. The story of David once again shows the distinction between worldly lust and unconditional love. The Bible records in the Book of 2 Samuel 11 that David, the King, was bored, leading him to the rooftop of his palace, where he saw a beautiful woman. He lusted after her, which led him to adultery—a resultant effect of his selfishness. Sequel to this action, because he craved more of her and wanted to own her for himself, he ensured that her husband was killed on the war frontline. In effect, what worldly lust births is sin, and the Bible records that as a man thinks in his heart, so is he. Hence, a lustful heart births sin, and the heart keen on sin cannot love anyone else in a Godly manner.

Ways By Which You Can Determine Whether the Sort of Love You Have Towards Your Partner is Worldly Lust or Unconditional Love

In the climate we live in, love and lust can sometimes have a similar look and feeling. The reason is they both start with having a friendly connection. However, before you go deep into building ties that last with your partner, there is a trite need to decipher whether the sort of attraction you both share is built on the foundation of unconditional love or worldly lust. Just like the Bible says in the Book of Psalm 11:3, if the foundation is destroyed, what can the righteous do? The foundation of your relationship with your partner matters a great deal. This is because it helps you to understand just what kind of relationship you share with your partner.

Remember, the basis of this narrative is to teach you about pearls in yourself that lead you towards the path of finding the sort of love that lasts for a lifetime. It is imperative that you are able to use your knowledge of the pearls in you to build an unconditional form of love with your partner built on the foundation of God's Words. Here are a few ways by which you can properly understand the distinction between unconditional love and worldly lust:

1. **Love Validates the Feelings of Your Partner:** I already mentioned that when you genuinely love your partner, you would feel connected with them in a way where their growth becomes your happiness. On the reverse side, their pain becomes your pain too,

because you want the best for them, even as your worlds are about to be united forever. The Book of Mark 10:8 (NKJV) says, *"and the two shall become one flesh; so then they are no longer two, but one flesh."* When you love your partner based on unconditional love, you will find that you are drawn to feel their moments because you two have become one, and whatever affects you affects them too.

2. **Working in Line with a Mutual Long Term/Short Term Goal:** Unconditional love with the one you have chosen to be your lifelong partner would make you decide on plans that align with you. This is because you both have agreed to be a part of each other's journey. If your relationship revolves around mutual goals and plans for the future, this indicates it is beyond mere worldly attraction.

    It is imperative to state here that setting mutual goals with your partner seems ideal. It is important to set realistic goals based on the plans you both had for yourselves before the relationship kickstarted. This is all the more reason why you should try to build a relationship that works based on plans and goals you set for it. Each of you should not neglect to work on such plans in alignment with each other's demands. An instance of how this plays out is with partners wanting stay-at-home wives and the woman wanting to work to earn her own money. A part of setting plans and goals based on this is to agree on the sort of job she would get. You both would have to reach an arrangement subject to slight compromises.

Realistically speaking, it matters a great deal to love your partner as they want to be loved according to their love language, even during the process of goal setting and making plans. The reason being it is easy to enter a state of love burnout when the relationship seems to be working but the personal plans of one or either party do not seem valid.

3. **Positive Feedback to Personal and Relationship Vulnerabilities:** Vulnerabilities are not always negative if there is a positive response to those vulnerabilities. There are many reasons people get vulnerable about their loved one. Most times, it is because of certain things they cannot control. For instance, you could get vulnerable about a loved one you are used to seeing and constantly making calls with when you do not see them for a day. This is valid, and there is no way you can control that

situation. Vulnerability also means insecurity. If anything, it could be a basis for talking about what you do not understand with your partner.

Constant communication is one-way unconditional lovers undermine the consistent insecurities that can arise out of situations they cannot control. Regarding insecurities and positive responses, the story of Nicodemus in the Book of John 3:1-21 comes to mind. The Bible records that Nicodemus met Jesus in the middle of the night. This singular action shows that he had been perturbed about a situation for so long that he could no longer hold it in himself. He was vulnerable about how best to serve God almighty. This led him to Jesus for the confirmation process of serving God. He asked Jesus about how he could be born again. Ideally, there was no obligation on the part of Jesus to give him a direct response. However, Jesus went on to state that he had to be born of water and the spirit to be born again. This kind of response gives redeemed hope. It also stems from a place of unconditional love.

When you say you love your partner unconditionally, your response to their vulnerable state should be able to put their mind at peace. This is because you care for them, and their feelings greatly affect you. In today's world, you find that utterances of supposed married people or those dating could mean conflicting ideas that negate the basis of a godly relationship. If your utterance when your partner needs assurances puts them in a precarious state, then it is most likely that your relationship wasn't built on unconditional love but worldly lust.

4. **Unconditional Love is Built Overtime:** Stating that the love of God is the foundation upon which unconditional love should rest makes a lot of sense. However, you need to understand that when two people decide to build a connection with themselves for a happily ever after sort of life, those two people come together based on their individual differences. It is just like having a best friend with whom you have mutual interests. The fact that you have a mutual interest with your best friend does not mean they do not have other traits in them which you don't have.

The Bible says in the Book of Amos 3:3, *"Can two walk together, unless they are agreed?"* You already know the answer to that rhetorical question. In essence, this means that, for the kind of relationship you would be sharing with your lifelong partner, you need to come to terms with the fact that there are differences you both have. This would be a basis for misunderstanding sometimes, but over time, a sense of agreement would beckon on you both. This is how unconditional love is built in a relationship. It is a feat that comes over time, and it stems from a deeper understanding that you both have become a team.

Note: The important lesson to learn about worldly lust and unconditional love, especially as the topic relates to your relationship, is that unconditional love is built on selfless love for each other. On the other hand, worldly lust is built on a selfish desire that satisfies the body's craving, as opposed to the spirit of God that you both are supposed to embrace.

CHAPTER SEVEN

The Difference Between Dating and Courtship

"Nevertheless, because of sexual immorality, let each man have his own wife, and let each woman have her own husband" (1st Corinthians 7:2 NKJV).

You would have to pardon me if I am wrong, but the old concept of dating before the word became as it is, is. You simply go out on a date just to meet with someone and probably get to know them. It is sort of an acquaintance meeting which could either escalate into a love situation or otherwise. Basically, I am speaking about how it used to be many years back. However, a lot of things have indeed changed in today's world. The idea of dating has gone far beyond what it used to be, including many immoralities. You find young ones going on a first-time date which is supposed to be to get to know someone else, and then it transcends into a first-time sexual situation.

People have become so lax about self-respect that immoralities have become the day's order.

Anyway, since our focus is building godly relationships and marriages that stand the test of time, the first thing to state in this regard is that a Christian relationship is expected to lead to marriage. When it comes to dating, it's important to focus on mutual feelings rather than just emotions. This is because dating doesn't always come with a commitment, and putting too much hope into it can lead to disappointment and pain. Instead of simply *dating*, aim for a *Christian courtship*. Christian courtship varies a great deal from what the world calls dating. This is because the foundation of this relationship is centered around the love for God through Christ Jesus. Hence, the first requirement for two people to be in a Christian courtship is that ***they are lovers of God***.

In order to conclude that you and your partner are lovers of God, the Book of Deuteronomy 11:1 has provided what should be the standard of your relationship. It says, *"Therefore thou shalt love the Lord thy God, and keep his charge, and his statutes, and his judgments, and his commandments always."* Hence, whatever Christian courtship you might be building with your partner, you must respect God's laws. One of the laws of God that your courtship should revolve around is the concept of sexual purity. It is so sad this has become abused in the world we live in. However, should you be intentional about building a Christian courtship, the rule of God says you must abstain from sex until marriage. You might be wondering where this is stated in the Bible, but the Book of Hebrews 13:4 states, *"Marriage is honourable in all, and the bed undefiled: but whoremongers and adulterers God will judge."*

Once it is hard to maintain and keep the laws of God in your relationship with your partner, you can agree you are no longer practicing what a Christian courtship stands for. Why? Because many things might have changed about the world, but the standard of God, which is the basis upon which a Christian courtship should stand, would never change.

The next step after the foundation of the relationship has established is to **ask God if the standing of that relationship is His plan for your life**. The reason a lot of marriages and relationships break down irretrievably is oftentimes because people run past the plan of God for their lives. They get carried away with the niceties of a person, the fact that they are appealing, and with vanities about people that they feel the plan of God no longer matters in their relationship. When things eventually go south, surprisingly, those who didn't make God the basis for which the relationship stands begin to blame Him. God is not a magician who changes all your bad wills to good because He can. Everyone lives under the mercies of God, but sometimes, you need to ask God for what He wants for you and find out if your plan aligns with that of God. The funny thing about asking God to show you His plans for your life, especially as it concerns to relationships, is you would always get speedy answers.

Prayer is one effective way to ask about God's plan concerning your intended relationship. The Bible records in the Book of Mark 11:24 (NKJV), *"Therefore I say to you, whatever things you ask when you pray, believe that you receive them, and you will have them."* God is more than willing to showcase His plan for your life, but the first rule, as highlighted above, must be respected. You must love God enough to believe in His unfailing ability to hear your prayers. Afterwards, God's plan through faith would be revealed.

The interesting thing about the revelation of God's plan for your life is that God does this in a plethora of ways. Have you ever found yourself in a situation where you are stuck with someone who seems to be a bad energy to you? Then instead of sending them away, you simply pray to God about it and mysteriously, they just lose the zeal to communicate with you, and that settles it? This is just to explain that God answers our prayers in mysterious ways. When you find yourself doubting the ability of God to answer your prayer request about His plan for your life, just look within and assess things. Your answer might just be a clue you have not been looking towards for a while. The ways of God are not like that of man.

The third steppingstone for a Christian courtship is to **find a mentor.** The purpose of a mentor here is not to teach you about how to be a couple. The purpose is to prevent you both from succumbing to the flesh's temptation. This is especially after you have heard from God concerning His plans for your relationship. The verse of the Bible that speaks so much detail about a mentor for a Christian courtship is Acts 14:23 (NKJV), which says, *"So when they had appointed elders in every church, and prayed with fasting, they commended them to the Lord in whom they had believed."* For the purpose of Christian courtship, it would be vain to say the human body is dead. The Bible says that he that thinks he stands should be weary, lest he falls. Hence, the presence of a mentor in the realm of your relationship is to remind you of the mandates of God concerning a Christian courtship. This reminder is to keep you both in check regarding those actions that are likely to make you both fall into the temptation of the flesh.

In the same vein, the mentors you should seek are not mere marriage counsellors. They should be leaders in the church who are abreast of the rules of God concerning a Christian relationship. The offshoot of the Book of Acts 14:23 is to the effect that the elders of the church who should be mentors for your relationship are those that guide you in line with the doctrines of God through His Word. Should you ever find yourself in a situation where you feel that what the Christian mentor is telling you is vague or contradictory, the first thing you should keep in mind is that just like the church's foundation is the message of *Jesus Christ,* the foundation of your relationship should also be *Jesus Christ.* Hence, if your mentor states certain things contradicting God's message for your relationship, then it might be time to seek another mentor.

One of the many powers you have as a child of God is the ability to discern spirits. This is why you need to be spirit-filled to ascertain whether the

Christian mentor's words regarding your relationship are in tune with the dictates of God for a Christian courtship.

The Differences that Exist Between Worldly Dating and Christian Courtship

There is a trite need to emphasize the differences between worldly dating and Christian courtship. I find this to be quite expedient because of the way the world is wired now. Many of our principles of chastity as Christians are beginning to overlap with the ideologies of the world, and over time, Christians have begun to have a misconstrued perception about dating and Christian courtship. The basis of this segment is to expatiate the core differences between the two terms so Christian couples can begin to use their pearls in Christ to edify and give more light to a godly relationship with their partners.

1. **The Priority of Marriage:** The one factor evident in Christian courtship that you would seldom find in worldly dating is the concept of commitment. Thinking about it now, you would agree that it takes much intentionality to embrace the idea of chastity and sexual purity. Both features are evident in Christian

courtship, and the end goal of such a courtship, clearly defined from the beginning of this relationship, is that the two parties plan to get married.

On the other hand, in the worldly sense, dating does not necessarily have to be based on an intention to marry. As evident in the world today, people date for many reasons. A common variant of dating in the worldly sense is when people say they are in an open relationship. I did a few findings on what this means, and I found it means people date so they can embrace other sexual partners. Meaning there is no commitment on the part of either party. This is possible in worldly dating, but it is not valid with Christian courtship.

Imagine going through the stress of abstinence from sex and occasionally meeting with a church marriage counsellor. The basis for doing this can only be because of a clearly defined goal. There is an African cliché that goes, when the purpose of a thing is unknown, abuse becomes inevitable. Christian courtship often leads to marriage because of the practicality of commitment that thrives based on a clearly defined goal—the desire to get married.

2. **Testing Waters:** In most dating cases, as opposed to Christian courtship, the parties involved are only testing waters. People merely dating have multiple partners. The reason for having each partner is to have a fallback plan in case one of the others disappoints them. In one of the earlier chapters herein, we discussed true love not revolving around the feeling of fear. However, with the instance I have just explained about dating, you should know that a person dating a significant other would have multiple partners because they are scared. This is why it takes a long time for people who are merely dating to introduce those they are involved with to their parents. So much fear and doubt revolve around simply dating someone, which becomes a stumbling block to building a real relationship that can stand the test of time.

On the other hand, the situation of things in a Christian courtship is such that when parties are sure about the plan of God concerning their union, everyone in the church knows the duo is in courtship and aims to ensure purity until marriage. There would be no need to hide things because their intentions are pure and are driven toward a realistic union that lasts a lifetime.

Note: Despite God's standard for the relationship He expects from us, His children, some Christians still indulge in worldly dating instead of Christian courtship. When you subject yourself with your partner to a Christian courtship, you must state that you have set that relationship before God. The institutions around that relationship would help you preserve the pearls in your life. It would also help your partner to protect the pearls in them.

When Christians subject themselves to worldly dating, it means they have compromised the standard of God and decided to go with the flesh. Some say they are sure they would not succumb to sin even though they know there is no guarantee in the flesh. Do not put confidence in the flesh nor underestimate it. When I hear devoted Christians talk like this, the narrative that comes to mind is the story of Peter when he denied Jesus three times. To all intent and purpose, he was fervent in serving God, but temptation has no boundary or respecter of person. He was so confident in his human effort, but by flesh shall no man prevail, so if you are a Christian and still indulge in worldly dating, there is a high tendency that you might fall to the works of the flesh.

CHAPTER EIGHT

Understanding Toxic Relationships and How to Break the Bridge

"For where envying and strife is, there is confusion and every evil work" (James 3:16).

When thinking mundanely about the word toxic, the first image that comes to mind is something that is likely to kill. Juxtaposing this imagery with the concept of love *is likely to kill the love you share with your partner.* Toxicity in relationships is rarely up for discourse in many counselling talks about marriage and living a happy life ever after. The reason being it is very hard to admit when you find yourself in a toxic relationship. Why? Because most people in a toxic relationship forget so soon about how much the relationship drains them, making them endure the stress and pain that comes with their partner. Well, don't get things misconstrued. It is said time in and out that in love, we sometimes disagree to agree. Hence, healthy quarrels are allowed because you both come from different backgrounds with diverse experiences. However, when quarrels with each other make it hard to see the light in the relationship, there is a high chance you might be in a toxic relationship.

Ways to Know if You Are in a Toxic Relationship with Your Partner

1. **Either of You is an Egoist:** While it is very hard to deduce that a person is toxic, the first evidence revealing that you or your partner might be toxic is when either of you is narcissistic. When the basis of the quarrel you both have from time to time is because one of you is selfish and always unwilling to compromise, then it means you just might be in a toxic relationship.

   In the same vein, if the basis for which one of you doing an action for the other is for an ulterior motive, then it is selfish and, thus, a toxic relationship. In giving proper context to the stance of God about how true lovers should interact with each other, the Bible records in the Book of Philippians 2:3-4

(NJKV), *"Let nothing be done through selfish ambition or conceit, but in lowliness of mind* (humility) *let each esteem others better than himself. Let each of you look not only for his own interests, but also for the interests of others."* One of the features that Jesus Christ showed during His earthly ministry was the virtue of humility. It was His humility that made Him wash the feet of His disciples. When you embrace humility like a girdle around your waist, you will not do things mainly for your own personal gain. Rather, your humility would tilt towards a selfless feeling for your partner.

2. **Being Unable to Make Necessary Compromises:** One of the many ways you can decipher whether or not you are in a toxic relationship is if either of you is unable to make compromises. Now, this might seem necessary at one point or the other. However, when the inability to compromise comes with some sort of drama every time, then there is a possibility you might be in a toxic relationship. What is funny is, in most instances when these dramas occur, it is the one who is toxic who goes round and round about how they do not want drama in the relationship.

The natural way that conflicts occur in a true love kind of relationship is for one party to compromise so there can be peace. It might take a little longer than the moment of the rift, but a compromise has to be made for peace to reign. If your partner tries to escalate an issue at every point, irrespective of how small or big the issue is, then it is most likely that you are in a toxic relationship, and God, not being an author of confusion, can definitely not be in that sort of relationship.

3. **Always Being Right:** Have you ever been in a relationship with someone who feels they are always right? On your own end, do you always end up apologizing for a wrong you clearly did not do? Well, this is a core trait of people who emit a toxic vibe. Toxic people are so full of pride they hardly see themselves doing any wrong. What is worse with them is they have some decoy good traits that you see, making you feel as though they are humble or good people by default. However, their inability to be accountable for their wrongdoings ends up ruining the relationship because it will transcend from a loving relationship to one that revolves around a mild form of resentment from the one who is always the victim.

Relating to how toxic energies can break down a relationship. The Bible records in the Book of Proverbs 16:18, *"Pride goeth before destruction, and an haughty spirit before a fall."* A part of what makes one a mature partner is their willingness to be accountable. When they are wrong, they admit it. If there is any excuse that makes their action logical, they find a simple way to communicate. Accountability in a relationship is very vital. This is because it shows your partner you are invested in what the relationship can transform into. This is how you know you are either in a love tie with your partner or in a toxic relationship.

4. **The Standoffish Personality:** Have you ever seen a situation where a person is resented by many people? From a distance, you might begin to assume those people are proud. Well, the back story could be because the one which is avoided is a toxic person. When someone is toxic, it is not just one person who figures it out. As a matter of fact, all of those who interact with such a person would know they are toxic, and this leads them to avoid this person. On the other hand, the one avoided does not feel remorse or guilt for people not interacting with them.

What am I trying to bring out? Sometimes, to figure out whether or not you are invested in a relationship with a toxic person, the assessment would not come from you. It is often said love is blind because the feeling of true love tends to becloud your judgment of your partner. However, if you find that people do not like interacting with your partner because they feel they are likely to cause a scene and your partner does not feel bad about this, there is a high chance you are in a toxic relationship.

5. **Playing the Victim Card:** We are all a product of the experiences we have had in the past. In one way or the other, our experiences shape our lives. However, if your partner is the sort of person who always refers to a bad past experience as a reason for being the way they are, they are likely toxic. The essence of this is to use their past experience to make you and those who interact with them their victims. They do this so seamlessly that people begin to feel guilty they acted in a way that reminds this person of their past.

6. **Lying at Will:** One thing which defines a toxic person's personality is that they lie at will. This

is regardless of whether or not they are right or wrong. They are drawn towards having an overriding comment on a topic. By the time people around a toxic person know they are a liar, it would have affected their personality to the extent that the only way people view this person is as a perpetual liar. If your partner is this sort of person, then it is likely they are toxic. It also means they are not great listeners, and this could aptly affect your relationship.

Talking about toxic relationships, the personality from the Bible who comes to mind is King Saul in the Book of 1st Samuel, chapters 15, 19 and 21. It was clear from the beginning that King Saul had a great personality; as a matter of fact, he was revered and adored by his subjects. At the time, he probably didn't know he had some toxic traits in him until he began to allow the praise chants of the people to get to him. It got to a certain point in his life when the praises of David were more than his, and he began to look for ways to harm David. As time would have it, God directed King Saul to go for a battle where God commanded that he kill every living thing there. He disobeyed God, which ruined his beautiful relationship with God.

A moral lesson that can be picked from this story is when a person is toxic, the toxic trait in them not only affects how people interact with them. It ruins everything beautiful that is ascribed to them. Toxic people are poisonous people by default.

Note: From all that has been said about toxic traits, you should already have your pointers if you are the sort who is considering an assessment of the kind of relationship you have with your partner. The plan of God for our respective lives is for us to have an abundance of peace. It is the reason why one of the names of Jesus is *the Prince of Peace.*

Thinking about peace from a very rational perspective, you would realize that no matter the abundance of blessings you may have in your life, if you do not have peace, it seems like all those blessings are cursed. This was reaffirmed in the Book of Proverbs 10:22. God's blessing makes you rich and adds no sorrow to it. God promises His peace that's above all human comprehension (Philippians 4:7). Hence, if your relationship is filled with all the toxic traits highlighted above, then it means you are in a toxic relationship that is far from what God wants for you. It also means it might be time to distance yourself from such a relationship.

The irony of toxic relationships is that the ones who are toxic don't always admit it until things have gone extremely bad. This is why in compliance with the Book of Psalm 1, God has advised that toxic people, just like wicked fools, should be abstained from. Why? They have next to nothing to offer to your life, and if you allow them, they are more than willing to destroy your life. It is glaring that you cannot help them, not when you are in a relationship with them. Sometimes, even the friends of these people cannot help them.

In addition, all of these might seem very easy when you are not yet married to a toxic partner. However, there are instances when one finds out long after a marriage they are wedded to a toxic partner. In that instance, the first thing you need do is understand that your mouth has to be fixed with Heaven. The Book of 1st Peter 5:7 says you should cast all your cares on God and He would hear you. God is the creator of your partner, and it is God who can change him or her. This might be the best time in your marriage to show that you truly love them.

Breaking Free from a Relationship with a Toxic Partner

A relationship with a toxic partner can be very difficult to break off from. This is because a part of you has been invested in them all along. Breaking off that part of you with them can be very emotional and draining. Separating from a toxic partner takes a whole lot of intentionality. Love for self is the first step that tells you that you need to break off from such a relationship. Yes, it might seem pleasing to others to stay stuck in that relationship but think about what could happen to you just because you are in that relationship. First, it starts with verbal toxicity. After a while, you both become drained of the affection and love that once existed. You both begin to panic over the sparkles that once were when the relationship started. It even gets bad in some instances when the one who loves more in the relationship grows into a state of negative obsession, and things keep growing from bad to worse.

1. **Making a Decision Based on Love for Self:** When it comes to breaking off from a toxic relationship, the basis upon which that break-off should occur needs to be premised on love for self. You need to understand that prior to

this toxic relationship you might be in, you had a life. Your life had been smooth and perfect before this person appeared. What is the worst thing you think would happen after you break that relationship? Each of you would continue with their respective lives, and probably even go on to find someone who matches the positive energy you both give.

We have spoken extensively about loving others and your partner in the same way you want to be loved. However, there are times in life when you just cannot help a situation. You need to be selfish for a bit at this point. Loving yourself more in this regard might seem selfish, but it is the right thing to do. You are more likely to move on from that relationship faster when you understand the basis for breaking off is that you want better for yourself and your partner.

There is a cliché that is common in many social discussions. It is: *You cannot give what you do not have.* Now, you know for a fact that you are a loving person who is more than capable of giving out love to your partner. However, you would not be in the best position to dish out the kind of love your partner wants if you were in a toxic space. It ends up affecting you, and if you cannot help yourself, you will become toxic to yourself and those around you.

2. **Defining Your Support System:** A support system would be needed after you have broken up with your toxic partner. The need for that support system is because a part of you would seek to fill up the vacuum your toxic partner has left you coping with. However, you must come to the right acceptance that the stage after breaking up a toxic relationship is not for denial of the pain and hurt you feel. If anything at all, it is for acceptance and for personal cleansing. This acceptance and personal cleansing would not happen easily if you do not have a support system that helps you get the right energy to carry on.

Research over time has been able to prove that when people have a support system after a breakup, it helps them to ease mental stress. This is why you need to have family or friends who understand your times and seasons. There is a time and season for everything in life as explained in the Book of Ecclesiastes chapter 3. You need to accept that the season and journey you are in, after the breakup from a toxic relationship, is for you to heal and develop the capacity to love yourself and love others.

Jumping the gun and not building a means of healing from the hurt you feel would only make you a toxic person in any new relationship you delve into. The reason is that the insecurities from your previous relationship would slow down your capacity to act as a loving partner in a new relationship.

3. **Accept the Law of Burnt Bridges:** Bridges are built to link two destinations together. This tells us by default that bridges are built with intentions that need to be followed to the letter. Now, when those who built the bridge decide they need to burn it, it also means there is an intention to totally disconnect the two destinations that were linked before. This is a law you should embrace at the first instance after you have decided to call it quits on that relationship.

   People who have suffered from heartbreak because of love ties would understand that after the relationship, a vacuum thrives in you. This vacuum informs your subconscious mind that you need to replace the one you have lost. Now, while you might not immediately be attracted to the energies around you, there is a possibility for a rebound should your ex-partner suggest it. It becomes a bit awkward after you have accepted that rebound. Why? Everything that exists in the relationship at that point is likely to be based on deceit. Both parties are trying their best to make things work, making you both extra careful. The way a perfect relationships work is not because they are perfect by default. It is because both parties have decided to live and accept each other based on the understanding of the flaws they have.

When you accept a rebound from a toxic relationship, you will likely end up being twice as hurt as you were when you decided to call it quits with your toxic partner. In any case, there is a high tendency that before you called it quits you tried to help your toxic partner get better. This would have been done one too many times and you reached the point where you realized you could no longer continue with that relationship. The question you need to ask yourself if you have a clinging thought to go back is, *if things didn't get better before, what could possibly change now?* It's time to let the toxic relationship go. Don't indulge in it anymore.

4. **Cut Off Every Form of Contact with Your Toxic Partner:** Many people say that cutting people off from your life is toxic, and it only goes to show how immature a person is. The truth is, sometimes, it is best to cut off a toxic partner you have broken up with. Why? By default, these sorts of people are manipulators. There's a slight chance they would engage you in a conversation and play the victim card until they get through to your weakness.

An assessment in America about why many women seldom leave toxic relationships is because a lot of women are weak. Many of these women have already left the relationship, but their toxic exes still have access to them because they didn't cut off all forms of contact. In plain words, there is no need to have contact with an ex who was toxic if you know your plan is to move on from the damage the relationship has done to you. It helps you to avoid being an unknown victim to the antics of your ex because, by default, toxic people are manipulators.

One of the many ways you can cut off your toxic partners from your life is to ensure that you block them from your social media accounts. Blocking them would prove to you and them that everything is over. It sets a clear boundary for the new kind of life you are more than willing to define for yourself.

5. **Making Yourself Understand You Deserve Better:** One of the many reasons you broke up from a toxic relationship is you deserve a better form of love. You need to constantly make yourself understand this. Why? Because one of the many ways your ex has held you back for so long is that they have made you believe that when you break off the relationship, you will never find anyone better than them. Well, this is a lie because you will always find someone in the universe who appreciates you for who you are. You need to constantly remind yourself of this fact, or else you will have a constant urge to go back. One of the ways you can make yourself understand this is to ensure you become your own mantra for healing and growth.

6. **Having a Constructive Plan for Your Healing:** One of the many ways you can move on from a toxic relationship is to plan how you intend to cope with the emotions that would fuel your world after the breakup. The essence of this is to improve one aspect of your life,

pending the time you delve into a new relationship. Developing an aspect of your life after a toxic relationship is one of the ways by which you can work on an already disrupted self-esteem. This is why you would find that people who break up from a toxic relationship sometimes find a way to go back to school or start working on their careers. It is because this makes them feel good about themselves and reiterates that they are worthy of something better.

At the starting point of making constructive plans for your life, you first need to ensure you have a documentary folder of your emotions. The reason for this is to assess the aspect of your life you need to work on. In assessing some people's lives after a toxic breakup, they find they are constantly depressed. This shows them they need a therapist's care. Knowing what you need to do after a toxic break up is another means of healing from the harm the relationship has done to you. It is also one of the many things you need to work on to make constructive plans for your life.

7. **Embrace Personal Positivity:** If there was ever a better time to embrace personal positivity, it would be at the point when you are

moving from a toxic relationship. Ordinarily, there are many limiting factors to you being able to maintain a positive persona. However, to move past this stage of your life, you need to embrace all sorts of positive energies that make you feel better. It could be a sport you love or your choice of food. At the end of the day, the aim is to ensure you do things that make you happy.

CHAPTER NINE

Why Do Breakups Sometimes Occur in Christian Relationships?

*"The Lord is near to those who have a broken heart,
And saves such as have a contrite spirit"*
(Psalm 34:18 NKJV).

The goal of a relationship for a Christian couple is that it ends in a marriage situation. When it does not happen as planned, it could be a reason to feel sad and depressed. This is a normal human feeling, but sometimes, even in the midst of a storm, there is a reminder in the Word of God that seems to assure us of a brighter morning despite the storm. The plan of God for our lives is that we live happily and thrive in the abundance of joy, and this is still God's plan for us despite whatever we might be facing at the moment.

While it might be hard to cope with the heartbreak, there are some notable reminders you need to have at the back of your mind to get past this mist of emotions.

Understanding Breakups as a Christian

While going through a breakup as a Christian, the first thing you need to have at the back of your mind is that you are human and it is okay to feel terrible about what has happened. Hence, you should allow yourself to be human at the moment. However, you need to also know if it was God's plan for your life, things would have been different. There is a lot you do not know about the cosmic world you live in. When certain things do not work out as planned, it might be God's way of trying to help you avoid a bullet set in place by the devil. Remember, in the Book of Isaiah 54:17, the Bible says that no weapon fashioned against you shall prosper. This does not mean the weapon against you will always be a physical weapon. Sometimes, it might come in the form of disappointment from a myriad of expectations you had. This is the reason why despite the trickle down of emotions you feel right now, you still need to trust the plan of God concerning your life. God's plan for you thrives on deep-ended love.

Why else would God ask that His son comes to the world to die for you? It is because He loves you. Do not allow this feeling to undermine the understanding of God's love for your life. If things have happened as it has, it is because God has better things set in place, all for your good.

Dealing with the pain that comes with heartbreak can be an arduous task. In most instances, there may be a drive in you for a rebound. However, the best thing you can do for yourself and your future partner at this point is to allow yourself to heal while waiting on God's set out plans for your life. We live in a social media world where it is easy to have a façade of what we crave out of life. In the quest of trying to fill up the vacuum your former partner has left, don't fall into the deceit that the world lives in. Rather than rush into a new relationship, dwell richly on God's Word, take out time to heal and pray for your next relationship. Quite interestingly, a breakup this one time might just be God's way of trying to allow you to pray for the marriage that would give you the invaluable peace and love you seek.

Furthermore, do not fall into the bandwagon of people who feel God is the reason for the mishap that befell their relationship. The Book of Psalm 145:9 says God is good all the time. God is never the reason the mishap that befell your relationship happened. Most Christian relationships that break off occur because of the place of sin in the life of the parties to the relationship. Sin is not a creation of God; it is the creation of the flesh that you cannot on your own volition overcome. Sometimes, sin in a relationship could unveil itself as a flaw or weakness that one party to the relationship finds they cannot cope with, which becomes a reason to let things slide. To overcome this in your next relationship, you need to consecrate yourself and be in tune with the dictates of God's Word. The Bible says that although your sins may be as red as scarlet, He would make you white as snow. Although your flaws may have made things pan out differently this time, God would never forsake you. It is up to you at this time to return to the Lord in prayer and confess the wrongs you might have committed knowingly or unknowingly.

There are two things that would probably come to mind while battling the emotions that come with a breakup phase as a Christian. The first is the feeling of shame that stems from what people would think of you. The second is the profile that people, especially those in a church, would ascribe to your personality. There is no denying the fact that the one sort of relationship the church loves to celebrate is marriage between two devoted Christians. Even in this phase, you should know it pays to love and lose it right now rather than to find yourself in a toxic marriage and then struggle to lose it. You know, thinking about it right now, there are a lot of commendable features King David had that made him the apple of God's eyes. If we did not go into details of all those features, we would have to agree he was one person who understood how to lean on God despite the circumstances he might find himself in.

When King David fell into the temptation of his flesh and sinned with Bathsheba, it was easy for him to get carried away with the profile that people would ascribe to him. Rather than see things from the perspective of what people would say, he chose to see things from the angle of being in sync with God. He understood that rather than seem right before humans that are in themselves sinners, he was better off making things right with his creator. This is the angle you need to focus on. Your breakup phase should make you seek more of God's face rather than lean on what people would say about you. In the end, what people say would not matter much. It is God's plan for you that matters the most.

While the pain might be understandable right now, you need to also know you cannot hate or detest your estranged partner because of the love of God. In admonishing the concept of love, the Bible goes as far as letting us know we should also love our enemies. In this context, your former partner is not even your enemy because, as a Christian, you are not allowed to hate people. God hates sinners, but even in the midst of so much sin, God still sent His son Jesus Christ to come to die for your sins because He loved you. This is the reason why you cannot hate your former partner. When all is said and done and the world has ended, when we all return to our heavenly home, your former partner, also a devout Christian, will be your brother or sister in Christ. You need to heal and create a space for a rooted love in Christ Jesus.

One of the things a lot of Christians tend to do when they are battling a breakup is to doubt the plan of God for their lives. They suddenly forget the verse in the Bible which talks about God making provisions for the birds of the air. They forget that if God makes plans for birds of the air who do not have a designated life like ours, He has a much better plan for us, His children. The Word of God says that whatever it is we want from God, we should ask and it would be given to us. This time in your life might just be the best time for you to ask God to give you a partner who gives you peace of mind and loves you just as much as you want to be loved. God is never too busy that He does not have the time to listen to the words in your mouth. You just need to have the consistency to ask God for what you want, and He will grant the requests of your heart.

There is an idea the devil puts in the mind of Christian devotees when a breakup occurs. It is that your partner is the one at fault. It is even more surprising that your friends might begin to ascribe faults to your estranged partner, and you have no choice but to stick with their words. It is how the flesh is wired to live in denial of the flaws that may be. We forget so soon that it always takes two to tango in a relationship. Hence, while your partner might have his or her flaw, there was an active role you played in it all. What you need to do at this point in time is to ensure that you focus on finding out ways your weaknesses undermined the relationship. You can even ask for the opinion of some friends and family members who are sincere and can tell you the truth. By the time you have been able to decipher those flaws, the next thing you would do is to go to God in prayers so He can grant you a change of heart and a means to make yourself better and avoid repeating what happened.

While it might be hard to believe those around you at this moment, you need to remember that Jesus died on the cross of calvary because of the sins of you and me. It is not possible that He doesn't understand what this moment of grief must seem like. If there is one thing that connects you with Jesus Christ as Lord and Savior, it is because of the pain you feel in this moment. Sadly, many Christians feel there would no longer be suffering when they accept Jesus as their Lord and personal Savior. Accepting this faith is knowing there will be trying times in this phase you are going through. You should also bear in mind that as much as you might be hurting right now, God has a plan for your life, and that plan would make you appreciate His faithfulness beyond this very moment of pain.

CHAPTER TEN

What Does It Entail to Have a Great Marital Relationship/Commitment?

"...I found him whom my soul loveth..."
(Song of Solomon 3:4).

If you are a Christian and you have had the time to go for one of those many marriage counselling sessions, you would have heard on more than two occasions about that aspect of the Bible that says the greatest of God's commandments is love. While this is a valid point for those who are married and still in a Christian relationship, it is essential to state that love alone does not keep a Christian relationship or marriage. Some other features need to be fused together to allow a Christian home to thrive.

While there is no direct roadmap to staying committed to a Christian marital relationship, the following are some qualities that many Christian couples have utilized to keep their marriage intact:

1. **Loyalty and Faithfulness:** If there is one line that everyone knows about Christian marriages, it is the line that deals with the aspect of exchanging vows, where couples promise to be faithful and loyal to themselves through health and wealth, sickness and in strength. This seems like mere words, but loyalty and faithfulness are almost as important to a couple as love is.

    At the inception point of a marriage, spouses are highly likely to love and trust each other. Why? Because they have not found each other in questionable situations with others. However, it is hard to maintain the relationship from the very moment that either of the spouses breaches the loyal and faithful vows of their marriage. You would find that many marriages are destroyed today on the hill of loyalty and faithfulness. Couples are beginning to forget their virtues, making them jettison the trust they could have earned from their partners.

    In speaking about the vitality of loyalty and faithfulness, the Bible admonished us in the Book of Mark 10:9, *"What therefore God hath joined together, let not man put asunder."* The institution of marriage is sacred and respected by man and God. In your prayer that you do not meet albatrosses in your marriage, it is also important to pray that you do not become the breaker of your own home because of the breach of trust and loyalty.

2. **The Virtue of Honor:** Many married couples don't quite understand that honor is vital for a marriage to thrive and stand the test of time. Respecting them is one way you can prove you honor your partner. If you respect your partner, you will refrain from doing things that deliberately hurt them or their personality. If there is one place where honor is lacking, it is in many celebrity marriages. Many of these people do things so the world can see. When the patches of their marriage begin to crumble, they start saying all sorts of things about their partners. This is not how a Christian marriage would thrive.

Respect is fundamental, and it has to start with each party to the marriage. It is just like they say, *respect is reciprocal.* Hence, if you want your partner to respect and love you, then you would have to love and respect them first. In corroborating this point, the Bible says in the

Book of Romans 12:10, *"Be kindly affectioned one to another with brotherly love; in honour preferring one another."*

Abraham is one personality in the Bible who I revere because of his respect for his wife. You would recall that Sarah had been trying to talk Abraham into sleeping with her handmaid. He refused on many occasions. He had to eventually lay with her out of respect for his wife. This was why at the point when she had to send the handmaid away from there, he was quite on the conservative side because he understood the vitality of honoring Sarah so their marriage could thrive.

3. **Being Humble:** Being humble is a feature that keeps Christian marriages. In a home where humility thrives, there would be no place for arrogance and pride. This is because humility is more accommodating to the opinion and interest of the other partner. Arrogance, on the other hand, is selfish.

Oftentimes, I have heard people ascribe roles in the home to men and women in marriages. This conception of things has bred the notion that we live in a man's world. The truth is, for spouses who love each other with all their hearts and might, they would be more focused on doing those things that make their relationship thrive. In such a home, there would be no need for shared roles because everything would be done out of love. The conception of shared roles is ego-wedging, which is pride on its own.

Similarly, humility in a marriage means you can be accountable for your actions. That is, when you are wrong, you are quick to admit you are wrong, and your partner is willing to do the same for the purpose of your marriage to thrive.

4. **The Virtue of Patience:** Patience is a virtue which spouses should embrace in their marriage. Everyone comes from different backgrounds with diverse nuances and experiences. However, the one way you can learn to accommodate each other is when you indulge each other in patience. If everyone has to be a bit hasty about everything, it might be hard to understand each other.

   Talking about the sort of marriage that thrives based on commitment, this does not mean there would not be rifts from time to time. It is just like we say, we disagree to agree. It means that even in those times when you disagree, the virtue of patience allows you to accommodate your differences so that you and your spouse do not blow things out of proportion. This is why I am of the view that it takes one who is humble to be patient. These two virtues work hand in hand.

The Bible says in the Book of Ephesians 4:2 that we should be completely humble and gentle, be patient, bearing with one another in love. Patience, as a virtue on its own, does better than bad in the light of so many situations that would occur at the blooming stages of your marriage.

5. **Being Understanding:** Flowing from all the other virtues that have been mentioned earlier, if you truly love your partner, it should not be hard to understand them. You both would have to understand that you come from two different backgrounds. Hence, the way you both would react to situations in life would be different. This is the reason why understanding as a virtue cannot exist on its own. Spouses also have the feature of empathy in them. You can only say you understand a person when you can empathize with the past experiences and events that have made them who they are.

Note: Finding the pearls in your partner is not just about loving them wholeheartedly. Sometimes, finding the pearls in your partner defines those attributes in you both that would help your relationship stand the true test of time. An assessment of your relationship from time to time would show you whether or not these virtues exist in your relationship or otherwise.

CHAPTER ELEVEN

The Fundamentals for a Successful Relationship

"This is My commandment, that you love one another as I have loved you" (John 15:12 NKJV).

A successful and healthy relationship with your partner requires a lot of intentional work. It is always an appealing sight when we walk down the alley that leads us home and a couple is sharing a memorable time with themselves in a garden at sunset. This is one of the many fantasies many of us have of what a perfect relationship should be like. It is not like a perfect relationship does not exist. Depending on what you consider perfect to be, it can be tempting. Temptation is not a sin but yielding to the temptation is a transgression. It is similar to the notion that when you have a disagreement, there is nothing wrong with having a disagreement but how you deal with it matters. It just requires a ton of work in progress. Before proceeding further into the exposition of the fundamentals for a successful relationship, the first thing on your mind should be that having a successful relationship has nothing to do with your past. It does not matter what wrong might have happened in your previous relationships. What matters the most is how invested and committed you are towards making your current relationship work out as planned. The Book of 2nd Corinthians 5:17 says, *"Therefore if any man be in Christ, he is a new creature: old things are passed away; behold, all things are become new."* Develop this kind of mindset to all your paths of life and you will be a winner. It is okay if the lesson you learned from previous experience, whether good or bad, helps to guide you in a positive way moving forward.

The first element determining whether your relationship with your partner will be successful is the kind of goal you both share. Partners ready to build something long-term would have no problems setting a common goal based on what they both have planned for themselves. However, to kickstart a successful relationship, some fundamentals should be evident. They are:

1. **Having a Sparkle of Emotional Connection with Each Other:** When it comes to having an emotional connection with your partner, the

goal is not to be in love with each other. The goal is to ensure that each of you feels loved with the other. When you both are in love with each other, it means you both can relate to each other's moments. On the other hand, when you are being loved by your partner, you can empathize with each other's moments just as you would want an ideal partner to interact with your moments.

For instance, when your partner feels sad because they lost their job, a part of making them feel loved is trying to be in their moment. You spend time with them. If it is possible to look for opportunities for them, you do it. If you can support them financially, then that is also an intentional act that shows your partner they can bank on you through the thick and thin.

2. **The Ability to Disagree Quietly:** A successful relationship requires the ability to manage disagreements. There is a proverb that says when two people enter a room and they come out with a glee of smile on their respective faces, it means they did not go in there to tell each other the truth. On the other hand, when two people enter a room and come

out frowning, then someone has told the truth to the other person.

A true relationship with the likelihood of standing the test of time would have both parties able to manage their disputes quietly and maturely. If you and your partner are in the habit of raising your voices at each other, the perception you would give those around you is that you have a toxic relationship. Having a discrete disposition when you both disagree is a mature sign that you are on to a relationship that would stand the test of time.

It is also important that you are not scared to enter into a conflict with your partner. Why? Because conflicts or disagreements are a way of venturing your thoughts and emotions about things you do not like. On the other hand, it gives your partner the avenue to get to know you better. No matter how much your partner loves you, they would not be able to love you enough unless they know you. This is why you should not be scared of having disagreements that validate your emotions.

3. **Understanding that Other Relationships and Interests are Valid:** One way to identify a toxic relationship is when it does not give you the room to be anything else outside of the

relationship. You would realize that in a short amount of time, you would become toxic to those who knew you long before the relationship. In the same vein, it is pertinent to state that mounting too much pressure on your partner can exert toxic energy which could end up ruining the relationship.

This is why you need to maintain relationships with your family and friends while with your partner. However, it is important to set reasonable boundaries with good understanding of the Scripture that reminds us that a man must leave mother and father and cleave to his wife (Genesis 2:24). This is keen to a solid relationship. If you are not careful, outside influences can contribute to the detriment of your relationship. While they love you, partners must know where their priority lies. The world would not always revolve around either of you. Getting to indulge your personal interests and spending quality time with your other loved ones gives you the capacity to be a better lover to your partner, and this would make the relationship linger for a very long time.

4. **Being Able to Communicate Effectively and Honestly:** One of the many ways you can

work towards a successful relationship with your partner is to be very expressive with your emotions. Research has shown that relationships where partners can communicate their emotions without fear tend to last longer than relationships that reek of many secrets. Communicating with your partner honestly makes them feel at ease with you, and it makes the bond between you stronger than ever before. This is how you build a kind of love so strong that it stands the test of time.

All You Need to Know About Maintaining the Love You Have Found with Your Pearl

When it comes to love and affection, it is easier to fall in love with a person than to maintain your love story with your partner. Interestingly, this requires conscious efforts and is not something God would come down from Heaven to help you with. I have been reiterating the need to be very intentional with your relationship from the very beginning of this book. On the wise, it makes a lot of sense to understand how best to maintain you love story. Why? Because an understanding of your love story would make you build a strong support system and a means of staying happy when life throws lemons your way.

There is no spark in the relationship of many because it was built to deal with emergency situations when they arise. When there are no storms, each party only focuses on other aspects of their lives, soon forgetting that what you nurture ends up blooming. Relationships are like plants; what you invest is what you get in return. If you do not invest intentional efforts into your relationship, you might find it hard to maintain the love you once found over time.

To become aware of how to maintain a successful relationship, the following pointers should be taken into consideration:

1. **Spending Quality Time with Each Other:** We live in a world where social media and the internet have really changed the course of things. Quite frankly, the internet has indeed made our lives easier, but at the same time, the internet has come to ruin certain aspects of our lives that should be endemic. There is no amount of communication with your partner via your cell phone that beats being able to physically spend time together and exhibit your emotions towards one another.

   Do you recall the first time you made up your mind based on God's Word that you would love to spend the rest of your life with your partner? There was an enthusiasm in you to want to know them and see their face daily, and complacency in maintaining that same energy just because you felt you knew them enough, and there was no way they could ever leave you. This is one way that many relationships go down the drain. Maintain the energy of seeing and spending quality time together, just as much as in the first phase when you both were getting to know each other.

There is a cliché that goes, *no matter how busy a person is, they can never be too busy for the ones they love.* We live in a clime where seeing face to face has been replaced with text messages and video calls. The happiness that comes with seeing each other can never be compared with a digital mechanism. It is different, and if communicating over the cell phone takes more priority than actually seeing each other in person, it is just a matter of time before the relationship dwindles.

Note: Spending quality time with each other should be a priority. You should also remember that the basis of your relationship is the foundation God has set through Jesus Christ, our Lord. Hence, it would be better to spend some quality time in an open space where you both would not be tempted to commit a sin that takes away the pearl in you both. The only exception to this is if you are married.

Just in case you are short on ideas of things you both can do while around each other, trying something new, like visiting a new restaurant, can be one of those bonding ideas for maintaining the love tie you have with your partner. Finding a hobby you both enjoy is another means of spending quality time with each other.

2. **Understanding the Need to Communicate Effectively:** When it comes to effective communication amongst Christian partners, it reeks of so much empathy. It is different from talking, which involves simply conversing with a person. When you meet up with your partner, you can both communicate about what you might be going through in your lives. There would be a perfect form of synchronism that continues to attract you both to each other. When the practice of effective communication begins to dwindle in a relationship, couples lose the drive to interact. While you both might not feel the impact on your relationship when

the going is good, this could have a major impact on your relationship when either party is stressed.

One of the ways by which partners can show a mastery of effective communication is when you both learn to communicate about what you need. It is easy to conclude that your partner is insensitive when you presume they should know what you need every time. However, when you communicate what you need, it makes them feel appreciated because you are telling them what they need to know so they can understand you better. Sadly, the reason a lot of couples leave things to the guessing game is because it is hard to talk about what one needs. They feel that talking about those things would only embarrass or send a wrong signal to their partners. This is not the right way to think about someone you share a relationship with. Talk to them; believe me, they want to hear from you too.

Another way by which couples can show a mastery of effective communication is by understanding nonverbal cues. People have many modes of conversations including body language. When you and your partner can understand nonverbal means of communicating with each other, it helps you feel loved and allows you to connect easily. On the other hand, when this nonverbal communication stops, discord begins, and it could affect your relationship.

3. **Understand You Cannot Always Have What You Want in a Relationship:** Life is often about giving and taking. If this saying is in the least bit true, then it means you would not always be on the receiving end of life. Sometimes, you would also have to part with something. This rule applies to a relationship. The way it works in a relationship is what is embedded in the 80/20 rule, which says that in a relationship, there is no such thing as a 100% mark for anyone. There are days when you would give 20% energy. In those days, your partner, in trying to make the relationship work, would give 80% of their energy, and vice versa. In effect, if you expect a relationship to be 100% of everything you have in your head, then you would set yourself up for disappointment in no time.

If there is one fact you need to learn now about maintaining a healthy relationship, it is that relationships are mainly about compromises. Compromises here do not mean you have to lose yourself all the time. It means you would have to meet each other in the middle on days when you cannot agree on an issue. This is how the best relationships thrive.

In understanding the *give-and-take* concept as it relates to relationships that work, it is important to state that both parties have to clearly express the things they prioritize. This is all a part of understanding what your partner wants so you can be abreast of what limits you would be willing to go to when compromises have to be made. They are expected to be more than willing to do the same for you. It is also important to state that with compromises, things do not always have to go your way. You could easily give off a toxic feeling when you always want compromises to favor you more. Make your partner feel that their wants are valued in the relationship too.

4. **The Principle of Situational Management:** Effectively managing situations is another way you can maintain the love you have for your partner. In this wise, you need to come to terms with the fact that you both come from different parts of life, with different experiences and means of handling situations. When the going is good, both parties

understand how to manage themselves. The problem, however, occurs when it comes to managing stressors within a relationship.

The first rule for situational management is you should take out your frustration on your partner under no circumstance. While the stressor might take its toll on you, you need to understand that your partner is not the problem. If anything at all, you both are supposed to be a team that weathers the storm together.

You should also know that trying to force out a solution to the problems you might be facing can cause more strain in your relationship. This is why you need to find a way to deal with the situation together. There is so much that can be resolved just by you both sharing moments of truth with each other.

CHAPTER TWELVE

Revealing Signs That Show If You Are With the Right Pearl (Partner)

"Submitting yourselves one to another in the fear of God"
(Ephesians 5:21).

If there is one thing I really love about the Christian faith, it is that the Word of God is a complete book that tells us all we need to know about varying aspects of our lives. Whatever you seek knowledge about, just go to the Bible and there is a Scripture which speaks to you in a way that nobody has ever done before. The revealing signs that show you if you are with the right partner are well stated in the Bible. Firstly, because the basis of your love for your partner is through Christ Jesus, it is imperative to state that the first sign that shows you if you are with the right pearl is that they love God. Now, the question is, *how do you know if your partner loves God?* Well, the answer is that man's ways are not the ways of God. When a person loves God, they would have a drive for those things that God loves. They would constantly want to seek the face of God in prayer, and they are cheerful givers by default.

The Book of 2nd Corinthians 6:14-15 tells you all you need to know about the right spouse. That portion of the New Testament tells you not to build a relationship that leads to marriage with an unbeliever. This makes a whole lot of sense. The story this brings to mind is that of Samson. Should Samson have hearkened to the Word of God and his parents regarding marrying someone from a strange land, the havoc that befell him would not have taken place. This shows you that, more often than not, when you become unequally yoked with unbelievers through marriage or a relationship, you are more likely to be corrupted. Hence, the right partner for you as a Christian is someone who loves God and is more than willing to do His will. Their love for God would always rub off on you, which is how a perfect relationship is built.

While it is great to understand that your potential future spouse would be a Christian who loves God, you still need to be careful. Why? The Book of 2nd Timothy 2:20 says, *"But in a great house there are not only vessels of gold and of silver, but also of wood and of earth; and some to honour, and some to dishonour."* The great house, as referenced here, is the house of God, and this Bible verse is connotative of the fact that in the house of God, you would find all kinds of people. Some come to serve God, and others come to make people derail from the service of God. At the end of the day, everyone comes into the vineyard of God to say they have come to serve God. This is why, as a Christian who intends to get married to someone who stays with them through thick and thin, you must have the ability to discern.

For one whom you would love to settle down with, apart from being able to pray about it and hear from God, you should also check how they showcase their love towards their friends and family. Those whom they relate with also matter. The truth is explicated in 1st Corinthians 15:33, which says, *"Be not deceived; evil communications corrupt good manners."* Those whom a person frolics with tell you a lot about their personality. How they treat those they claim are their friends also gives you as much information as you would need to decide if they are meant for you. Why? How they treat their loved ones shows you a glimpse of how you would end up being treated. Those whom a person relates with also have an influence on such a person. This is why you need to be able to discern on all fronts which personality you would love to settle down with.

Another revealing sign that shows if the pearl you have found is the apt fit for your life is their understanding of the church's doctrine. Oftentimes, a lot of Christians seem to feel that what makes two people incompatible is whether they are Christians or not. On this yardstick, many denominations would say a Christian should not marry a Muslim. In addendum to this notion of things, it is also important that Christians who do not share this same perception of the belief in Christ Jesus should not get married to each other. Apart from a conflict in the belief system, it also affects many other issues that may arise should the relationship ever lead to the marriage phase.

Understanding if you are ready to be committed to one person is another sign to take note of after you have confirmed the status, personality and position of your partner regarding a marriage union. While relationships require a lot of work, marriages also require a lot of work, and what is more, is that marriages ordinarily should last a lifetime, so the work that needs to be done would be forever. This is why you need to decide now if you will continue to be someone's husband or wife forever. Many Christians do not understand the sacrifices that come with being married to one person forever, which is one of the major reasons marriages fail today.

In addition, you must have been able to decipher if you are ready to be this person's spouse. The ideal thing to do is get a marriage counsellor with water-tight experience who tells you all there is to know about life beyond the early marriage stage and going on your honeymoon. During discussions with the marriage counsellor, you talk about how you run the home, the kinds of jobs you would be doing, and the act of splitting bills.

The last sign that shows you that you have been able to find the right partner for yourself is the drive to seek the face of God concerning this journey. The Bible says in the Book of Proverbs 3:5-6, *"Trust in the Lord with all thine heart; and lean not unto thine own understanding. In all thy ways acknowledge him, and he shall direct thy paths."* You both need to have that drive to pay God for this new journey you are about to embark on. The ability to bring God early enough into this union goes a long way to show how God would be invested in it. Trust God!

PART C
ESTABLISHING LOVE ON GOD'S OWN FOUNDATION

CHAPTER THIRTEEN

Understanding Your Pearl (Partner)

"Husbands, likewise, dwell with them with understanding, giving honor to the wife..."
(1st Peter 3:7 NKJV).

Have you ever had a moment in your relationship when you had an automatic thinking mode about your partner and you were right? If so, then the ability to have that automatic thinking mode about your partner stemmed from an in-depth understanding. Personally, I have met with couples at varying points in time when I had a conversation with the husband first and then later on when I saw the wife, her response to the topic of discussion was similar. This analogy also comes from a wealth of understanding.

Understanding your partner means you have known them to the point that you could easily explain what their actions and the intent behind those actions mean, and you would still be right. The advantage of understanding your partner is it reduces the chances of misunderstanding and the inability to communicate effectively. Sometimes, communication for such spouses could mean just a gesture, and their partner just gets them.

Seeing couples get married and live the best time of their lives for a very long time can be very appealing, but the truth is, the ability to live together for years requires an interpersonal understanding between the partners.

The first step towards understanding your partner is *to understand yourself.* Understanding yourself means you are aware of your emotions and you can control them. Ultimately, this rubs off on how you treat your partner's emotions. When you understand your emotions, you can checkmate them in tune with your partner's. This helps you both to develop a top-tier relationship.

Making the act of understanding your partner a priority is one of the ways you can get to know them better. By default, you cannot understand all there is to your partner, but when you are intentional about it, it becomes easier to understand them. This conscious step might take quite some time, but the end goal of building quality relationships would be derived.

Understanding your partner's body language cycle could also be another means of knowing your partner. At first, when they move their body in response to an event or action, it might be easier to deny that their body language didn't affirm or negate the action. However, if you are quite observant, you will be able to read the meaning of certain body language because of the cycle of responses your body gives over time. It could be a smirk, a shrug or their countenance. The aim is to figure out what it means.

Another way you can understand your partner's personality is to **ask questions about their past**. The truth is, our experiences, especially from the past, say a lot about how we operate in our present or future relationships. When you ask questions about your partner's past, you would gain a better understanding about why they react to situations in a certain way, which would help you to know how to accommodate them when you find out they need your care and support during certain moments.

Appreciation, when your partner shares certain details concerning their lives, allows them to be vulnerable around you. This would allow them to share more details with you, enabling you both to have an enhanced relationship. At times when complimenting your partner means you value them, allow them to connect with you with the same form of energy you have shown them over time.

Understanding the communication pattern of your partner also helps. Some people feel comfortable sharing their personal stories with the use of words. They can be very blunt with you concerning certain moments in their lives. Understanding how your partner likes to communicate would help you relate well, and this facilitates a more peaceful and cordial love situation.

There are times when **walking away** is a means of communication. During those times when you both disagree on certain topics, rather than hurl accusations at your partner, if you choose to walk away, you would realize that it gives enough forum for quality reflection on points you both have made. It also gives enough room to apologize when needed, which helps you both have a more mature forum for loving and caring for each other.

CHAPTER FOURTEEN

Learning to Love One Another — Never Compromise Your Values Again

"But put ye on the Lord Jesus Christ, and make not provision for the flesh, to fulfil the lusts thereof" (Romans 13:14).

When you compromise, it means you are willing to relinquish the extremities of your personal standards to accommodate that of your partner. Compromise is a necessary skill for spouses when they find themselves in a love or marriage situation. It gives a valid ground for choosing peace above being right. A case of compromise in the Bible is in the story of Daniel with his three friends. They didn't compromise their love for God because it is a no-brainer to relinquish the place of God for human validation.

The Bible does not allow us as Christians to compromise the place of God in our lives. This is why the Book of Deuteronomy 5:32 (NKJV) says, *"Therefore you shall be careful to do as the Lord your God has commanded you; you shall not turn aside to the right hand or to the left."* While it makes a lot of sense to compromise for the sake of peace in your marriage, the standard that God has set for us as Christians is just and right, and God would not condone us having to bargain on those principles to be right in the sight of man. It is an addition to the Bible portion that says what would profit a man to gain the world and lose his soul? We all remember the story of King Jehoshaphat and King Ahab. King Jehoshaphat's compromise with the wicked King almost cost him his life. The story of Jezebel is also another admittance of how God does not want us to compromise His standards in our lives.

One of the many reasons Christian couples compromise in their marriages is to please their spouses and those around them. The fear of what may happen if they do not compromise is why it becomes so easy for them to compromise. They forget it was God who had created them, and if God didn't make their lives perfect as it is, there would be no reason to compromise on any ground.

While it makes a lot of sense to compromise based on personal preferences, it does not make sense if you have to compromise your personal principles, standards and moral codes. This is why there is a need to accept the place of God in your life. Once you cannot compromise with the love of God in place of worldly lust, it becomes easy to maintain God's standard, and it is on this basis you would choose to not compromise because it would mean picking the world over the love of God.

Certain Values You Must Never Compromise in a Relationship

1. **Don't Compromise with Your Personal Goals:** One of the ways by which you know your partner loves you immensely is that they become supportive of the core of you. When they are supportive of whom you are, it becomes easy to love them because whatever goals you both might set for the relationship would be in acceptance of your personal values and goals. A relationship that wants you to change who you are or the plans you have for yourself outright is not the best form of

relationship for you. We find this variant in some marriages where women are told to be stay-at-home wives, neglecting their career goals and dreams because they need to conform to their husbands' desires. This is not so bad, but you become a shadow of yourself when your goals no longer mirror your life.

The path of compromise can only be reached when both partners are willing to forego certain dreams so their union can thrive; not outrightly relinquishing personal goals in such a way that a relationship makes one partner a human with no purpose in life.

2. **Don't Relinquish Quality Ties With Friends and Family Members Because of a Relationship:** As stated earlier, the purpose of a relationship is to support what both partners stand for while working on something that can stand the test of time. A partner who is supportive of you would never allow you to let go of ties which have, over time, defined who you are. Your family and friends have been your love and support system long before you met with your partner. If you both need a support system, these are the same set of people who can help weather through the

storms that your relationship may face from time to time.

Hence, do not allow your relationship with your new partner to cause you to let go of quality ties because you would not be able to retrace the ties once you have lost them.

3. **Never Let Go of Your Belief System Because of a Relationship with Your Partner:** The story of King Solomon comes to play out here. King Solomon married many women and let them practice their strange gods' service in his land. It didn't take too long before his love for vanities led him astray from the love of God. Whatever relationship you have with your partner should respect your personal belief system. In any case, a Christian relationship should exist on a mutual belief system. Hence, your relationship or marriage with your partner should not turn you away from the love of God. Why? Because it is the foundation upon which a perfect love story exists.

What could go wrong if you do not compromise the love of God in your relationship? Nothing. If anything, it allows the standard of God to direct the path of your relationship with your partner.

Reasons Why You Should Not Compromise Your Personal Values for a Relationship

1. **A Reduction in Personal Integrity and Self-Trust:** You should not let go of your values in a relationship because it would make you begin to doubt your sense of personal judgment. This is because all you stand for would already be taken away from you. This means that in instances when you have to take a stance for what is right and true, you would not be able to have a firm ground because you no longer have your own values. In some instances, it would make your partner begin to doubt your ability to decide when it comes to taking a stance that can dramatically change the course of your relationship.

2. **Your Words Would Amount to Nothing:** Relinquishing your values gives off the impression that you are not a man or woman of your own words. Hence, when you say you would do certain things, even beyond the context of your relationship with your partner,

people begin to doubt you, which affects your relationship with those around you.

3. **Mental and Emotional Starvation:** When you relinquish your values for the purpose of your relationship, you would feel a sense of emotional and mental drainage. It would affect your capability to love your partner as they ought to be loved. In some instances, it might affect your ability to love your partner based on the energy they introduce into the relationship. This could even quickly make you a toxic person as you begin to emit some energies that work against the relationship.

CHAPTER FIFTEEN

Take Charge of Your Life—The Fundamentals of Living and Loving the Right Way

"Owe no man anything, but to love one another: for he that loveth another hath fulfilled the law"
(Romans 13:8).

The plan of God for your life is that you live in an abundance of love and life. God didn't create you to live a life of misery. The essence of the coming of Jesus Christ to the world is to give you renewed hope in life. Hence, taking charge of your life and being able to love effectively is the basis for which God has created you in His image. During the earthly ministry of Christ, all the miracles performed by Him were to remind you of the kind of life that God expects you to live.

Ways By Which You Can Live and Love in Compliance with God's Word

1. **Understand the Concept of Self-Love:** A Latin maxim says, *Nemo Dat Quot Non Habet.* This means you can only give that which you have. Deep in your mind, you would love to be the sort of human capable of loving others. However, there is no way this can be possible if you don't embrace self-love. The concept of self-love would show you that there are some things you should not settle for. For instance, a toxic relationship. There is no way you would love yourself and decide to settle for a toxic relationship that drains you from seeing and accepting yourself for whom and what you are.

   The concept of self-love is also very useful, even when you are betrayed by those you love. It is the reason why the Bible tells us that sorrow may last for a night, but joy comes in the morning (Psalm 30:5). Self-love would allow you to see the essence in yourself so you can keep hope alive until you get what you seek. The concept of self-love also teaches you about the ***golden rule: do unto others that which you would want to be done to yourself*** (Matthew 7:12). Hence, you would find that when it is convenient to love or otherwise, you are more than willing to dish out love. Why? Because it is how you would rather be treated by your partner or those around you.

2. **Be in Control of Your Mindset:** There is so much your mind does to you. A person with a negative mind will likely end up having negative realities. This is because the mindset you have shapes your reality. When talking about the Christian faith and its impact on your life, you would find the nature of God in your faith. The nature of God, as buttressed in your faith, is for you to have a positive mindset. A positive mindset is a growth mindset. A growth mindset sees beyond the situation to the truth you so keenly sought.

3. **Don't Indulge Worries, Fears and Anxieties:** Have you ever wondered why most of the scary images in your mind seldom come to reality? It is because anxiety, fear and worries are figments of your imagination. You only give life to those negative thoughts when they begin to direct your actions. The wrong thoughts that you have, viz a viz their impact on your actions, produce the negative life you may get.

Being scared and worried about your relationship can be very logical because you have been hurt before, and if you had your way, you would want to prevent a repetition of those sad events. But taking a cue from the rise of Jesus Christ after He died on the cross of Calvary, if He had leaned so much on the pains He suffered on the cross, would there be hope for a renewed life that His resurrection gave? No!

The plan of God for your life is that all things will work together for your good. Why? Because you love God. Being insecure about your relationship or marriage is an indirect way of doubting that all things will work together for your good. Let the worries and fears go. God has got you now.

4. **Practicing Gratitude:** One of the many reasons people don't get to appreciate the essence of God in their life is because they look amiss. They become fixated on what they want God to do for them, now and here, that they forget they exist. To be able to live and love life more dearly is a creation of God. God has a ready-made plan for your life, and it is in the spirit of gratitude that you will be able to accept God's plan as being good and perfect. Practice gratitude and appreciate God for the life and love you have.

Conclusion

Swine and Pearls is a relevant, and an on-time narrative that speaks directly to every relationship, especially those who are seeking relationship on a long-term basis. Discussing swine and pearls is a unique thought-provoking way to raise awareness of who you are, who deserves your association and whom you create a bond with. It is a reminder to the self that there are innate virtues in you that are valuable and must be protected with high esteem. If you fail to embrace them, and become careless, you can easily be abused and a product of Matthew 7:6.

Pearls within the context of this book are those virtues that God has bestowed on you to make you a special and loving being. The nature of God that He has instilled in you is love. When you can love your neighbor as you love yourself, it is a good start to strike a relationship.

The concept of self-relationship matters a great deal when it comes to building a love that stands the test of time. After you have perfected that respect for self, you will project the same onto those you encounter.

Building true love on the foundation of God's Word is exactly how God wants you to nurture a love life with your partner. Therefore, the concept of Godly relationships is different from worldly lust. The kind of relationship that thrives on the Word of God for your life is selfless and unconditional. It is a kind of love which develops based on a sense of commitment that leads to marriage. On the other hand, a swine mentality full of worldly lust is a selfish form of infatuation which many mistook for love. Partners in a worldly form of relationship only get to know each other for selfish and sinful reasons, so they will eventually be crushed, broken, and destroyed. Living a fulfilled life with your pearl should rest on the promises and commandments of God concerning your life. The Book of Jeremiah 29:11 (NKJV) says, *"For I know the thoughts that I think towards you, says the Lord, thoughts of peace and not of evil, to give you a future and a hope."*

TEN DAYS OF INTENTIONAL PRAYER AND MEDITATION

"Blessed is the man Who walks not in the counsel of the ungodly, Nor stands in the path of sinners, Nor sits in the seat of the scornful; But his delight is in the law of the Lord, And in His law he meditates day and night" (Psalm 1:1-2 NKJV).

Meditation is a very potent tool given to us by God. Sadly, we do not utilize or embrace it to get the benefits. Meditation must be practiced to help us obtain clarity both mentally and emotionally. It helps us to calmly focus on the Word of God. by engaging our minds to reflect on that which we have taken in. In the Book of Isaiah 26:3, God's Word says that He will keep in perfect peace, those whose mind are stayed upon Him because they trust in Him.

Prayer is vital to all successes in every area of our lives. In the Book of James 5:16, we are reminded that the effectual fervent prayer of a righteous man avails much.

Day 1

Swine and pearls are a biblical expression of a metaphor for who you are. The Scripture states that you should praise your creator because you are fearful and wonderfully made. It is incumbent upon you to preserve your glorious being. Sadly, many have chosen to defy their inner beauty by adopting the nature of swine. Therefore, you are admonished to be vigilant and guard the gem God placed in you, which makes you a pearl. It is imperative that you identify yourself so you can attract the same kind of partner. There must be compatibility in your relationship. There should be mutual natural agreements based on your core values. The two of you must agree before you take that special walk.

Meditation Prayer

Dear Lord, I pray I will be the glittering pearl You have created me to be. Lord, I am imperfect, but You have allowed me to grow in Your Words. They are light and life. Your Words are precious, out eternity, from everlasting to everlasting. My obedience to God's Words will ultimately define me to be as a swine or a pearl. I pray in Jesus' Name, Amen.

Day 2

"The Lord is my shepherd; I shall not want"
(Psalm 23:1).

When you acknowledge the Lord as your shepherd, you surrender your whole life to Him and give Him total control over you. On the other hand, you accept that you are His sheep, and sheep are known to be beautiful but not brilliant. In this case, it is perfect to be a sheep in the hands of a good shepherd. Sheep have been seen grazing by the wayside, fulfilling the needs of their appetite, and often unmindful of danger. Sometimes, you are steadfast in your desire to be filled without thinking of the long-term effect it can have on you. This is when the excellent shepherd shows you a safe pasture or a better way. The good shepherd wants you to be filled, whole, healthy, and protected from annihilation. The eyes of your Shepherd are on the sparrow, and He keeps strict watch over His sheep and supplies their needs. Do not worry about what He didn't give you. Instead, be content with what you have today and anticipate what it will be tomorrow.

Meditation Prayer

Heavenly Father, help me to understand the relationship between a good shepherd and a sheep. I know that You only have good intentions for my desired fulfillment and for my soul to prosper and be healthy. Help me not to wander away from Your pasture where there is everything I need to be safe and satisfied. In Jesus' Name I pray, Amen.

Day 3

"He that loveth not knoweth not God; for God is love"
(1 John 4:8).

Love is the greatest virtue that can be found in any human. In the Book of Matthew, Jesus was provokingly asked by a lawyer, what is the greatest commandment? He responded, *"Thou shalt love the Lord thy God with all thy heart, and with all thy soul, and with all thy mind…Thou shalt love thy neighbour as thyself"* (Matthew 22:36-39). Here is where the whole essence of love begins and ends. This means you must love yourself to treat someone else like you treat yourself. Jesus says these are the two greatest commandments and they are the railroad on which any successful love and lifelong relationship can be achieved. Meditate on these things.

Meditation Prayer

Dear Heavenly Father, please help me understand the only way to know and experience the great love I seek. The way to love is through You and in me the ability to reciprocate that love You freely give me. My pearl has become my friend, lover, and life partner. Help me cherish and perfect Your love in me so I can share the love with my spouse and friends in their perspective place. In Jesus' Name I pray, Amen.

<u>Day 4</u>

"All scripture is given by inspiration of God, and is profitable for doctrine, for reproof, for correction, for instruction in righteousness" (2 Timothy 2:16).

All things are possible through Christ If you trust in your understanding, you know you will fail. The Lord is your strength, your sustainer, and your guide. Your total dependance is on Him. None who trust in God shall be ashamed. God promises to order your steps in His Word. His Word is true and faithful and cannot fail. God puts more value on His Word and esteem above His name in Psalm 138:2. God gives all Scripture and is helpful to teach you what is true and makes you realize what is wrong in your life. It corrects you when you go wrong and leads you to do what is right.

Meditation Prayer

Dear Lord, please help me to understand the effect of words and their power. Sometimes words are used lightly, and they do bring much hurt to others. Please help me to be cognizant of my words and weigh them before opening my mouth. Your Word states in Proverbs 18:22 that death and life are in the power of the tongue and they that love it shall eat the fruit thereof. Lord, please help me to manage my anger and patience. Help me to be tempered by Your Holy Spirit. In Jesus' Name I pray, Amen.

<u>Day 5</u>

"If any of you lack wisdom, let him ask of God, that giveth to all men liberally, and upbraideth not; and it shall be given him. But let him ask in faith, nothing wavering. For he that wavereth is like a wave of the sea driven with the wind and tossed" (James 1:5-6).

Wisdom is a virtue of a good life. No man should live without it. God tells us that if any man lacks it, let them ask who give liberally and without reproach. In times like these, when so much evil is happening in and around us, we need His grace to carry us through. He promises He will be with us and help us to make it through. Wisdom makes one wise. King Solomon demonstrated a perfect example in 1st Kings 3:16-28. When two women gave birth, one of the women slept on her child during the night and the child died. She came to claim the other woman's child. King Solomon had to judge the situation and use God's intervention to find the right solution. The woman whose child died was willing for King Solomon to cut the other baby in half to prove the living child belonged to her. Wisdom spoke loud and clear. King Solomon concluded that the baby belonged to the woman willing to save her child by giving it to the wicked woman who slept on her baby. He concluded that the living baby belonged to the woman who spared the child from being cut in half, which equaled death.

Meditation Prayer

Dear Lord, I pray for wisdom to operate wisely when situations arise. Let me fear You and Your Word. You declare that the fear of the Lord is the beginning of wisdom. Let me not live as a fool. Please help me not to destroy anyone with my actions or words. Give me good judgment in all things. In Jesus' Name I pray, Amen.

Day 6

"Study to shew thyself approved unto God, a workman that needeth not to be ashamed, rightly dividing the word of truth" (2 Timothy 2:15).

The Oxford Dictionary defines knowledge as fact, information, and skill acquired by a person through experience or education; the theoretical practical understanding of a subject. The Scripture announces that a lack of knowledge is a dangerous ground to travel on. It is highly destructive. God is saddened when He looks at His people and sees the foolish ways they appropriate in this life. This is what God said about lack of knowledge: *"My people are destroyed for lack of knowledge: because thou hast rejected knowledge, I will also reject thee, that thou shalt be no priest to me: seeing thou hast forgotten the law of thy God, I will also forget thy children"* (Hosea 4:6). Timothy could not have said it any better. You must study to show yourself approved so you can divide God's Word truthfully and not be ashamed.

Meditation Prayer

Heavenly Father, hollowed be Your name. Your Kingdom come on earth as it is in Heaven. Please grant me the desire to seek and obtain knowledge. Help me to study Your Word so I can be a tool in Your hand. Fill me with Your Word and remove annihilation far from me. I humbly take Your instruction, bind them around my neck, and hide them in the inward part of my heart so that they will be my guiding light to steer me into great triumph. In Jesus' Name I pray, Amen.

<u>Day 7</u>

"In all thy ways acknowledge him, and he shall direct thy paths" (Proverbs 3:6).

Wisdom is a principal thing but in all thy ways get understanding. It is the uttermost blessing when you have Godly insight to comprehend all matters. Experience gives you a sense of awareness of the feelings of others. It helps you to be sympathetic, tolerant and forgiving. Having a good understanding allows you to be a better problem solver. You will be slow to anger, provide soft answers that will turn wrath away, and have faster compassion. The Scripture says, *"Let this mind be in you, which was also in Christ Jesus"*

(Philippians 2:5). Understanding will help you to demonstrate those traits of our Lord and Savior. Understanding brings peace and shows love and respect. With it, you will be nonjudgmental and be able to restore great friendships and relationships.

Meditation Prayer

Dear God and Father of making, I praise You, the God of all wisdom. You said if any man lacks wisdom, let him ask of God that giveth all man liberally, and upbraideth not, and it shall be given him. You further state that it shall be requested in faith and that he shall not ask anything wavering. Lord, You say when I weaver, I am like a wave of the sea that's driven and tossed. You also say a double minded man is unstable in all his ways. Help me to be rooted and grounded in Your unfailing love. In Jesus' Name I pray, Amen.

Day 8

"Death and life are in the power of the tongue: and they that love it shall eat the fruit thereof" (Proverbs 18:21).

The words which come from your mouth must be seasoned with salt. Therefore, you must be intentional about them. Your words speak volumes. They should represent your heart. The

Scripture states that out of the abundance of your heart your mouth speaks (Matthew 12:34). Your word must be your bond. This is one of the ways you are known. You will be identified whether you are and can be trusted depending on how well you keep your word. You must endeavor to speak what you mean and mean what you say. Let your nay be nay and your yea be yea. Do not take your words for granted. God wants for you not to have vowed at all than to vow and not fulfill it. It is wrong not to keep your words or promises.

Meditation Prayer

Dear Lord and Savior, I come to You in the Name of Jesus. I ask You to forgive me for taking my words for granted. My words carry effects. I realized that my words could destroy or bring life to the hearer. Lord, please forgive me for my careless words and unkept promises; because of negligence, others are disappointed and hurt by my commitments. Lord, I repent and apologize to anyone I have broken with this nonchalant habit. Lord, help me to change how I treat my spoken words. Let them reflect You. Lord, help me to think before I speak or make any decision. I pray in Yeshua's Name, Amen.

<u>Day 9</u>

*"And be not conformed to this world: but be ye
transformed by the renewing of your mind, that ye may
prove what is that good, and acceptable, and perfect,
will of God"* (Romans 12:2).

The mind is the most formidable dynamic of all humans. It can make you or break you. No surprise that the Scripture admonishes us in Romans 12 to renew our minds daily to experience a total revolution. This means you will become a new person in your thought man daily. It suddenly makes sense and has become more apparent why you must quickly deal with issues of the mind, including anger, and not allow yourself to carry over matters to another day. Paul in Ephesians 4:26-27 tells us we should not let the sun go down on our anger.

The mind is one of the most influential and valuable tools for a successful relationship. The mind can be extremely unruly at times; however, you must bring it under the subjection of the Holy Spirit. You can take every thought captive, especially if it's not in line with what God says. You must be conscious of the ideas that come to mind and do something about them before they enter the heart. The mind controls both the flesh and the spiritual aspect of your life. From experience, the one you feed more will be in dominant control of you. The mind is so precious that you are encouraged to guard your mind and have the same sense Christ Jesus possesses. The purpose of Christ is to please His Father and to do His will. This should also be your goal.

Meditation Prayer

Dear Father Yahweh, I humbly bow before You sincerely, asking You to help me to be Your diligent servant. Father, only You alone can control the mind by letting the Holy Spirit temper it. I am admonished to have a pure, renewed sense every day. Oh God, I pray Your Word will be my mind trainer. You said in Your Word that I must set my mind on the things above which means the spiritual things, and I will reap eternal life; on the other hand, if I put my mind on the fleshly thing, I will reap corruption. Thank You, Lord, for the power You gave me over my mind. I can cast down vain imaginations and everything that exalts himself above You. God, I provide You with prominence to have control over my mind. As a human, I like to think that I am the good one, forgetting that so a man thinks, so is he. Lord, I need Your help to take authority over my mindset. In Jesus' Name I pray, Amen.

Day 10

"A man that hath friends must shew himself friendly: and there is a friend that sticketh closer than a brother" (Proverbs 18:24).

First, show yourself to be friendly if you need a friend. Be the best friend you can be—faithful, loyal, compassionate, trustworthy, available, and ready to lend a hand when needed. People are not interested in how much you know but in how much you care. It is always best to show transparency and authenticity. In friendship, a bond is usually formed depending on the company's level. Remember, it takes a friend to hurt or bring down a buddy. In today's world, many do not take friendship seriously enough, so it takes nothing for those you deem to be your friend to abandon you. The Scripture tells us that a friend will stick closer than a brother. Think about that; it means a lot. It speaks volume. If this should happen to you, remember you have a hero in you. Be encouraged to take Jesus as your friend regardless. He is a true friend. He will never leave nor forsake you, no matter what. All He requires is for you to be faithful to Him.

Meditation Prayer

Dear Lord, thank You for good friendship. Thank You for the means of excellent companionship. No man is an island. No man stands alone in the world You created, and You looked at it and said it was good. Lord, when You looked at man, You realized something was missing, and You said it was not good for man to be alone. You took a rib from Adam and made Eve. They were bone of bones and flesh of flesh, perfect in design, fit for each other. Lord, please help me to understand the true essence of good friendship and companionship. Help me to be the best version of true love and dependable friendship. Thank You, Lord, for providing friendship in You so everyone can have a friend by their side. Thank You, Lord, for helping me to be that dependable friend. In Jesus' Name I pray, Amen.

Questions and Answers

It is interesting to know of some reasons why many today are unhappy in their marriage. Let's take a look at different individuals and what they say.

One individual put it this way: Their connection to the marriage they are in was based on a friend who thought they knew a handsome gentleman or a beautiful young lady who was a somewhat single and trusted friend. They introduced them and out of that came a relationship that led to marriage. After a while, everything turned sour. This individual talked about the abandonment they experienced in that marriage. They spoke about the disrespect, dehumanization, loneness, and the psychological and emotional abuse they suffered during this so-called marriage. This was a long and unfruitful journey. It is said the best of their life was lived wasted. The only matchmaker should be Jesus. This is a common mistake many people make and end up entering the array of their life.

Question: What do you think about getting to know your mate through someone else's eyes?

Answer:_____

_____

_____

_____

Here is another scenario: Meeting your spouse through ungodly friends. There is bound to be a crash! I believe that their intentions were good, nevertheless, the Scripture reminds you not to walk in the counsel of the ungodly. There are many funny reasons why lots of humans fall prey and find themselves in a pit hole. Sometimes, an individual's situation pushes them to go out of line of what they really believe. That's the first red flag on your side. I know the rationality is vast and that does not make it right. The reason you should not let this happen to you is sometimes they move on to living their beautiful life because they know what they want and go searching for it while you are left in the dilemma they plunged you into. You cannot see your happy ever after through someone else's eyes. Wait and your eyes will see the special one. There is an instinct, a sense you feel when a good and godly connection is made.

Question: Who are your counsel friends of influence?

Answer:_____

_____

_____

_____

Never think you are so poor or needy that you need a man or a woman to help you out. That is the biggest mistake you could make.

Don't believe the first person who shows you some form of affection and hands you a glass of soda is the one for you.

Never think you are too lonely to carry on so the first one you meet, you think that's your last chance. NO!

Don't you dare think time is running out on you so you believe like a swine that the first water you see, you must wash.

A friend of mine once told me that he was in love with this individual. Somehow, the individual was not all that interested in him. He said he was so in love with that individual, he didn't know he could live without her. When the relationship ended and he looked back, he realized he was now the happiest camper because it did not go the way he originally wanted. But a straw that broke the camel's back was he observed how that girl would eat a cow and her calf and how embarrassed he would have been with her around his friends, and maybe he would not have been able to feed her. He is now happily married to a well-balanced Queen that can represent him anywhere. Learn to pay attention to individuals you connect with, especially if you are looking for your pearl. You know who you are and what you are looking for. Funny but true story.

Question: Have you ever seen swine with pearls around their neck?

Answer:_____

_____

_____

_____

This kind of uncontrolled behavior breaks up relationships and will make you unhappy.

Don't let your current situation dictate your choosing. It is extremely tempting but resist it. Like the saying goes, a drowning man can catch a straw but that doesn't mean he will be saved. The remedy is if you can't swim, stay away from deep waters. You may look and see others out there, but, as they say, the cat and the dog do not have similar luck. Don't be driven by your own passion in your pursuit of finding your gem. Seek God in your endeavor to find your pearls. It will happen in God's timing. If you can't trust God to work it out for you, He can't trust you to give you His precious pearls. Think about it. Many mistakes that have been made by so many people were due to lack of patience. Another reason for failure in finding a life partner is unpreparedness. Many times, you have not taken the time out to be a well-rounded individual so you find you have fallen short in areas as it relates to marriage, and it can cause an imbalance and even end up in separation.

It is imperative to enter into pre-marital counsel before you say I do. It is not to be taken lightly. Counsel can save your day and your marriage. When individuals think they are in love, they have a propensity to overlook all the necessary importance that is the real deal in a marriage. You find that the other party is doing their thing the way they like, not considering you. In situations like this, if you are not intentional about your relationship, you can find that marriage breaks down and keeps on going downhill until there is nothing left to bind the relationship together. In this instance, one party may try to save the relationship when the other party moves on. Even though you may be living under the same roof, it becomes a cover up and you begin living in the shadow. Marriage can be saved when both parties want to save it. Honesty is the best policy when one party does something that affects the other. It must be discussed in a timely manner. Don't wait for failure to happen then accuse the other party of breaking the marriage when you never discussed the issues you were uncomfortable with.

Third party interference is dangerous to any relationship including your marriage. This can happen in various ways intentionally or unintentionally. Be careful not to put anyone before your spouse. This means you must set boundaries, be smart, be intentional, and be cautious. You will have friends, but you must be mindful at all times of limitations. You cannot show more commitment to others on the outside and barely show any affection or commitment to your dearly beloved at home. Sometimes, it happens in church, work, or at play; it doesn't matter. This is one sure way to make your spouse begin to feel and think all types of thoughts. It is a natural tendency of humans. These kinds of behavior will cause problems in your relationship. Wisdom is a virtue. Individuals on the other hand must show some amount of responsibility and respect when interacting with others. Know how far you can go. It is always best to shun the appearance of evil (1 Thessalonians 5:22). Let wisdom speak.

Past relationships must be handled in a Godly, honest way with consideration for the other half in your life. Unfortunately, life throws humans lemons at times, including being married and divorced. If you should ever get married to another individual, it is imperative to show respect, and be intentional and sensitive to the relationship. Certain avoidance is necessary to set you apart from previous relationships and the present one. While you cannot be malicious to past relationships, you cannot still be so close to your ex, nor still allowing them to have so much power in your life they get anything they need without discussing it with your present partner. You cannot allow past relationships to counsel, dictate, or interfere in your present union. Make sure you let go of your past marriage or intimate relationships. Don't allow it to mess with you and your future progress. Always remember, the person on the other side of the spectrum is human. Don't give or create reason for doubt. Discipline is a virtue. Temptation is a force to reckon with. Never let yourself lose, thinking you can and will pass the test. Don't let it happen. Temptation comes in many ways. You may think your spouse is not seeing or hearing your conversations, but secrets have a way of coming to the light. This all comes down to your maturity, loyalty, respect, and diligence.

Extended family is a number one killer of marriage. Again, this comes down to setting boundaries. In Matthew 19:5-6, God specifically declared that, in a marriage union, a man shall leave mother and father and cleave to his wife and the two shall become one flesh so that they may be no more twain but one flesh. Do not take this aspect of Scripture light. You will be held accountable for this. There is no rationality about it. God has spoken. Your extended family will always be part of your life, nevertheless, they cannot hold priority in your life. You cannot go on doing secret business with them without the knowledge of your spouse. It is okay to help but not without your spouse's knowledge. When you begin to hide and do things outside of your marriage, it is a strong indication that something is wrong and invites the spirit of deception, selfishness, and alternate motive. If you invest in buying a home or property or anything with your extended family including your children, sibling or even friends without wanting your spouse's knowledge, you will open a door for the enemy to break up your matrimonial home. In other words, you would be making preparation for yourself with the intention of deceiving your spouse. Whatever preparation is made should be between you and your partner. Think when you go to your family, let's say at the time of your retainment, where would your spouse go? What preparations have you made for your married union?

Here are some things to consider talking about during your dating or courtship period:

1. Sex
2. Money
3. Family and children
4. Career
5. Paying bills
6. Vacation
7. Religion

8. Family values
9. Education
10. Ministry
11. Friends
12. Anything else you deem important to maintaining a Christian marriage

Here are some things to keep in mind while building a relationship with your spouse:

- Never let sex be your only motive to get married. There is much more to it than that.
- Don't get married to an abusive person then expect to experience love and affection.
- Don't marry a shoemaker then expect a doctor's attitude or behavior out of them.
- Be ready to take responsibility for your actions.
- Do not ask how God could let this happen to you. He did not do it. You did.
- Build a rapport with your spouse.
- Be each other's best friend.
- Communication is best understood by talking, not only action.
- It is of utmost importance to pray together.
- Get to know what makes each other tick.

- Know each other's love language.
- Be sensitive to each other's feelings.
- Husbands, remember you are the covering for your wife.
- Wives, remember to submit to your husband.
- Avoid temptation by training yourself to choose your partner every day over and over again.

About the Author

Pastor Vendrix Headley has been an ordained minister of the Gospel of Christ for decades. She ministers through songs, spoken words, radio broadcasting, and is a published author and the editor of the "ARYZE" Gospel Magazine. Vendrix is a passionate servant of God who loves to counsel and encourage those who encounter difficulties and are challenged in some way or other and feels a sense of giving up because of the gigantic giants they're facing. She is a strong believer in leaving our footprint in the sand. She rests on the Scripture that states a good man leaves an inheritance for his children's children (Proverbs 13:22). She believes in empowering others and willingly obeying what the Lord inspired her to do, imparting wisdom. All praise, glory and honor to God.

Vendrix is available for seminars, conferences, retreats, and any other speaking engagements. She can be reached via email at aryzenow@gmail.com.

Books written by Pastor Vendrix Headley are available for purchase from her publisher at writtenwordspublishing.com/vendrix-headley, via her personal website at vlove.us, and worldwide wherever books are sold.

Be on the lookout for other books
by Pastor Vendrix Headley:

When Destiny Calls Trouble Answers
Smile In the Tears
God's Hurting People (Revised Edition)

www.ingramcontent.com/pod-product-compliance
Lightning Source LLC
Chambersburg PA
CBHW071355120626
46546CB00002B/693